LOOKING EAST

LOOKING EAST

A CHANGING MIDDLE EAST
REALIGNS WITH A RISING ASIA

SHIRZAD AZAD

Algora Publishing
New York

Library of Congress Cataloging-in-Publication Data —

Names: Azad, Shirzad, 1977- author.
Title: Looking East : a changing Middle East realigns with a rising Asia /
  Shirzad Azad.
Description: New York : Algora Publishing, 2020. | Includes bibliographical
  references and index. | Summary: "Major Middle East nations are looking
  east, seeking to forge closer ties with the quickly rising Asia. This
  may represent a new sort of geo-magnetic reversal, as this time the
  poles flip from West to East, with potentially the same shocking
  reverberations of a North-South polar reversal. This work reviews the
  "Look East" approach of Iran, Israel, Turkey, Saudi Arabia, the United
  Arab Emirates, Iraq and Egypt"— Provided by publisher.
Identifiers: LCCN 2020040914 (print) | LCCN 2020040915 (ebook) | ISBN
  9781628944341 (trade paperback) | ISBN 9781628944358 (hardback) | ISBN
  9781628944365 (pdf)
Subjects: LCSH: Middle East—Foreign relations—East Asia. | East
  Asia—Foreign relations—Middle East. | Middle East—Foreign economic
  relations—East Asia. | East Asia—Foreign economic relations—Middle
  East.
Classification: LCC DS518.14 .A933 2020 (print) | LCC DS518.14 (ebook) |
  DDC 327.5605—dc23
LC record available at https://lccn.loc.gov/2020040914
LC ebook record available at https://lccn.loc.gov/2020040915

Other Books by the Author

East Asian Politico-Economic Ties with the Middle East: Newcomers, Trailblazers, and Unsung Stakeholders (2019)

Koreans in Iran: Missiles, Markets and Myths (2018)

Quo Vadis Korea: The Last Custodian of Confucianism and Its Atypical Transformation (2017)

Iran and China: A New Approach to Their Bilateral Relations (2017)

Koreans in the Persian Gulf: Policies and International Relations (2015)

Table of Contents

PREFACE

The present book sketches the looking-East approach pursued by major Middle Eastern countries over the past several decades. The study concentrates on the contemporary situation, with reference to critical historical developments in order to contextualize the current dynamics. The research is divided into seven chapters, each one focused on the looking-East policy of just one Middle Eastern country.

Chapter 1 focuses on Iran. As counterintuitive as it may at first seem, Iran embarked upon a policy of looking East long before that became a prevailing trend. However, since the importance given to this objective waxed and waned with successive Iranian governments, largely based on the country's domestic needs, some aspects did not receive adequate attention or failed to live up to their potential. Nonetheless, despite the uneven results so far, looking East is going to continue to be a pillar of Iran's foreign policy approach to the outside world for decades to come.

Chapter 2 argues that looking East has breathed new life into Saudi Arabia's modest foreign policy long characterized by strong attachment to Western countries, the United States in particular. Despite their explicit intention not to replace their pivotal Western allies with Asian partners, the Saudis have fostered closer connections to the East in virtually every area. The Saudi looking-East push has, moreover, dovetailed neatly with an equally salient reciprocal interest.

Chapter 3 examines how the Emiratis have in recent years strived to forge multifaceted relations with Asia in spite of the fact that the linchpin of the United Arab Emirates' (UAE) politico-strategic objectives rests on keeping close connections to a small number of countries in the West and the Middle East. Aiming primarily to secure its own growing economic and financial interests in a resurgent East, the UAE seeks to enhance its regional standing by serving as a stepping stone to help the rising Asian powers move into the Middle East. Much to the advantage of the UAE, the Asians are also increasingly capitalizing on the Emiratis' looking-East initiative in order to secure their growing interests in the region and beyond.

In Chapter 4, the study evaluates Iraq's looking-East record in the post-Saddam era. Lacerated by many years of devastating military conflicts and crippling international sanctions, Iraq lacked the financial and technological resources to rebuild its war-torn country. And since Iraq was left twisting in the wind and the West did not commit itself to a thorough program of reconstruction and development as widely expected, the Iraqis had to fill the void by turning to the East. By embarking upon a looking-East approach, therefore, Iraq aimed particularly to persuade a number of rich and resourceful Asian countries to enter into close cooperation with Baghdad. Many Asian countries were equally interested in rekindling their connections to the post-Saddam Iraq at a critical time when Western investors and businesses were holding back, thus leaving open potentially unique opportunities for new partners to put money into the sectors most conducive to their long-term interests.

Chapter 5 argues why Turkey's recent outreach toward the East has aimed to strike a subtle and nuanced balance between the country's new politico-strategic identity and its growing economic and technological requirements. Since the triumph of the Islamists in late 2002, Turkey has embarked upon a looking-East orientation, aiming to diversify its foreign allies and partners by engaging in multifaceted relationships with many Asian countries. Viewing the partial detachment of the Turks from the West as an important victory for the East, almost all Asian countries have also been interested in paving the way for Turkey to pursue its looking-East objectives.

Chapter 6 probes how Israel has embarked upon a looking-East orientation in earnest during the past several years despite its close alliance with the West over the last seven decades. Aiming to cultivate connections to almost all countries across the Asian continent, the new Israeli approach has strived to enhance the Jewish state's relationship with the East in almost all political, military, economic, financial, technological, and even cultural areas. Many Asian nations have also displayed a keen desire to expand their growing interactions with Israel, smoothing the way for the Israeli looking-East push to carry through its main objectives and overcome potential setbacks.

Finally, Chapter 7 investigates why Egypt in spite of its long relationship with Asian countries has been late in embarking upon a looking-East orientation in the post-Mubarak era. In sharp contrast to Cairo's previous political and military connections to Asia, however, the new looking-East inclination of Egypt aims primarily to gain some immediate economic and financial rewards from fostering closer ties with a number of resourceful and rising Eastern powers. Moreover, the Egyptian approach is in tune with some critical politico-economic objectives of those Asian stakeholders, giving Egypt a significant role as a bridge to link the East with the African continent. The chapter then concludes by showing why such a growing nexus would become even more crucial if the government in Cairo could make the most of its geopolitical and demographic advantages and enhance its desirability among an increasing number of Asian investors and entrepreneurs.

Shirzad Azad

Chapter 1. Iran: Rhetoric, Reality, and the Staying Power of Looking East

The political entities of East Asia, including for the purpose of our discussion greater China (comprised of mainland China, Taiwan, Hong Kong, and Macao), Japan, South Korea, and North Korea, have all played an indispensable role in Iran's external interactions as well as in its domestic circumstances over the past several decades. This development has massive ramifications for Iranians in the short and long term, yet academic studies on the topic have, for the most part, remained sparse and scattered. Still, a great deal of the relevant literature about Iran's multidimensional connections to East Asia, particularly the materials available in the Persian language, is pretty well encapsulated by the concept of "Looking East." After all, the looking-East notion in Iran was primarily about Tehran's relationship with the East Asian countries of China, Japan, and the two Koreas, though the concept has often been used to imply a similar connotation with regard to the recent foreign policy orientation of many other countries across the world as well.[1]

Looking East has certainly been a powerful framework for grasping certain elements in Iranian interactions with the outside world in the last several decades. Iran was among the first countries in the world to look east from the 1970s onward, turning the concept into a "guiding principle" enabling many interested observers to evaluate the purposes and performance of certain parts of the country's actions beyond its sovereign borders. Of course, looking East was not yet *à la mode*; as a new dynamic in inter-

---

[1] John Calabrese, *China's Changing Relations with the Middle East* (London and New York: Pinter Publishers, 1991), pp. 9–11.

national politics, in most countries it had yet to become a pillar of foreign policy or a common buzzword among policy experts and commentators.[2] Even in Iran itself, it took some time before "looking to the east" emerged as a convenient label. Political leaders, diplomats and analysts had yet to clearly formulate the concept; and some Iranians conceived it more broadly to include Tehran's orientation *vis à vis* Russia and all the countries located in South and Southeast Asia.

If looking east, in fact, was a crucial part of Iranian foreign relations for decades, why did the concept not attract corresponding attention? What lies behind the subtle discrepancy between what looking East was supposed to be about, in Iran, and the actual policy the country executed during that time frame?

Ideational intricacies: Looking East in rhetoric and practice

Looking East is, by and large, a recent phenomenon around the world. Now even major Western European countries such as Germany and Britain are no longer skittish about it.[3] And while the former is fixated on the potentially huge politico-economic gains to be found by looking East, the latter is impressed by significant socio-cultural benefits such as upgrading math scores and other educational standards that might derive from some Eastern experiences.[4]

This rising trend has to do with the massive increase in the weight and status of China in tandem with the gradual yet inexorable economic, military and diplomatic decline of the West, especially the United States. Whether the aim is to build new diplomatic and political alliances reflecting the shift in the power balance in the world, or merely to secure lucrative financial and business transactions in the near run, the rise of China has grabbed the attention of the whole world, to such an extent that many nations are now obsessed with how to gain more by forging closer connections to Beijing in political, economic, technical, military, and cultural areas. Today, looking East stands, first and foremost, for making the most of what China can offer, whether in terms of short-term gains or for longer-term strategic objectives.[5]

---

[2] Martin Jacques, *When China Rules the World: The End of the Western World and the Birth of a New Global Order*, second edition (New York: Penguin Books, 2012).

[3] Klaus von Beyme, "Redefining European Security: The Role of German Foreign Policy," in Carl C. Hodge, ed., *Redefining European Security* (New York and London: Garland Publishing, 1999), pp. 165–179.

[4] "Britain Turns to Chinese Textbooks to Improve Its Math Scores," *The New York Times*, August 5, 2017.

[5] "Shijie xiang dong kan—guoji renshi he haiwai huaqiao huaren rushi shuo" [The World Looks East—International People and Overseas Chinese Acknowledge], *Xinhua*,

Iran is primarily interested in the long run. Although the Islamic Republic is credited with inaugurating Iran's looking-East approach, some elements of the policy came into view in the pre-Islamic Republic era when the Pahlavi dynasty vowed to create a "second Japan," particularly in the aftermath of the first oil boom of 1973. The Iranian looking-East tendency had, there- fore, a longer period of gestation, starting before the Chinese embarked in earnest upon their policy of "reform and opening-up" (*gaige kaifang*) in 1978. In the decades that followed the establishment of the Islamic Republic, looking East was to play a considerable role in laying the foundations of a lasting relationship between Tehran and its counterparts in East Asia. In one decade, political and military objectives upped the ante, while economic interests and technological requirements gradually emerged to play a strong role in Iran's growing partnership with East Asia in later decades.

Still, it is a major misfortune that the Iranian predisposition to look East did not live up to expectations. As in Malaysia, under Mahathir Mohamad from the early 1980s onward,[6] the looking-East approach in Iran could have been geared toward learning more about what was really going on in Japan and the other four crouching "Asian Tigers," and gaining a deeper under- standing of their cultures, before China moved to emulate their successful model of development and economic growth.[7] A successful looking-East orientation in Iran, if it had been embraced wholeheartedly and implemented carefully, would have inculcated in the mind of many Iranian citizens the values of hard work, frugality, saving, and living within one's means. There were certainly many other valuable points, both at the micro and macro levels, to grasp while displaying looking-East propensities, but at the least a genuine attention to and good understanding of these constructive mores could, in turn, have helped the Iranian society to boost its efficiency, produc- tivity, creativity, and innovation. A true looking-East approach in Iran should have brought forth such valuable outcomes so that the country could reap the lasting rewards of its long-term and close connections to East Asia.[8]

The looking-East orientation in Iran would have had a better chance of fulfilling those core objectives in the long haul, moreover, if the people

---

February 24, 2018.

[6] Mahathir Mohamad embarked upon a policy of Looking-East soon after he became prime minister in 1981. He served as Malaysia's 4th and 7th prime minister from July 1981 to October 2003 and from May 2018 to March 2020.

[7] Ronald Dore, "Japan in the Coming Century: Looking East or West?" in Edward R. Beauchamp, ed., *Japan's Role in International Politics since World War II* (New York and London: Garland Publishing, 1998), pp. 23–30; and "Mahathir Reorients Malaysia," *The Japan Times*, July 14, 2018.

[8] Robert R. Bianchi, *Guests of God: Pilgrimage and Politics in the Islamic World* (New York: Oxford University Press, 2004), p. 124.

responsible for the policy had had skin in the game. If the elite policymakers and their advisors were truly intrigued by what was going on in East Asia, looking East would certainly have led to more much better outcomes for successive generations. This would have required a powerful coterie of individuals who had gleaned first-hand lessons from modern developments in one or more of the East Asian countries. Such a group of people would definitely be more effective in commanding a looking-East approach if its core members could speak an Asian tongue, enjoy Asian cuisine with gusto, and keep in regular contact with friends and counterparts in East Asia. But a major problem with the Iranian experience was that the authorities who planned the policy and put it into practice had little such experience and knowledge.[9]

Thus, Iran's looking-East approach was hardly a pre-planned, comprehensive policy designed to achieve specific goals within a certain timeframe. The orientation often got more traction under special circumstances such as the arms requirements during the Iran–Iraq War of 1980–1988. On other occasions, when Tehran was about to mend fences with the West, some of the people in influential positions were not sure the country needed any looking-East approach at all.

Iran has never abandoned its looking-East approach, however, and the country's steadfast attachment to this policy has delicately waxed and waned under different conditions. Still, Tehran ultimately favored material elements over ideational gains while boasting about or beefing up its looking-East credentials. In fact, looking East was to serve as a convenient contingency of sorts, assisting the Islamic Republic in muddling through one chaotic decade after another, roughly from the early 1980s onward. Even those soft aspects of the looking-East approach which had less pecuniary attributes were ineluctably affected by the way the Iranian government perceived and handled its counterparts in East Asia over the past several decades.

Politico-strategic stakes: Oscillating rhetoric

It may sound counterintuitive, but the first true venture in the Iranian looking-East approach coincided with the time when the newly-established Islamic Republic launched a staunch political campaign of "neither the East nor the West."

---

[9] "Iran Upholds South–North Equi-Distance Policy: Mansouri," *Korea Herald*, January 26, 1989, p. 2; and William R. Polk, *Understanding Iran: Everything You Need to Know, from Persia to the Islamic Republic, from Cyrus to Ahmadinejad* (New York: Palgrave Macmillan, 2009).

The "East" at that time meant the Soviet Union-led communist bloc, but the giant communist China was also a major stakeholder of that disunited association. Ironically, the Chinese, as well as the communist North Koreans, were soon to be courted for the urgent war requirements stemming from the ongoing internecine conflict with the neighboring Iraq, in the face of all anti-great powers and anti-communist pomposities promoted by the Islamic Republic's dog-whistle politics.[10] Beijing in particular had its own legitimate reasons for ignoring the political slogans in Tehran, while ungrudgingly lending a helping hand to the neophyte rulers of Iran. China was locked in a fierce geopolitical rivalry with Moscow; they were influenced by the strategic significance of Iran, no matter what type of political system or ideology ruled the country; and, most importantly, there were huge and badly-needed material benefits to be secured through military, and other types of, cooperation with the new Iranian authorities.[11]

The main architect of the Islamic Republic's first chapter of looking East was actually Akbar Hashemi Rafsanjani. He played a very instrumental role in carving out and implementing Tehran's foreign policies toward East Asian countries, especially China and North Korea. Throughout the war period, Rafsanjani made several trips to East Asia, during which he laid down some basic foundations of Iran's long-term connections to the region. Once the war came to a grinding halt and Rafsanjani took the helm of the Iranian presidency, looking East would serve a number of non-political and non-military objectives as the post-war reconstruction plans called for a closer economic and technological relationship with East Asian states, especially Japan, South Korea, and Taiwan. Surrounded by a pliant and sycophantic cohort of Western-educated technocrats and liberal-leaning ministers and advisors, Rafsanjani was hardly a diehard proponent of deep ties with the East in the long run. Still, his half-hearted fondness for the East was almost always blended with pragmatism, and that is why his looking-East legacy survived, *mutatis mutandis*, long after he left the office of the presidency in 1997.[12]

Under the Khatami presidency, political as well as cultural themes took the center stage as Tehran's foreign and particularly domestic politics were engulfed in contentious ideational and non-material squabbles. Iran was officially in favor of a fuller engagement with the wider world, but the continuation of international constraints forced it to talk and act selectively. Looking East certainly retained its appeal, but it was now only one of

---

[10] Thomas Parker, "China's Growing Interests in the Persian Gulf," *The Brown Journal of World Affairs*, Vol. 7, No. 1 (2000), pp. 235–243.

[11] John Calabrese, "From Flyswatters to Silkworms: The Evolution of China's Role in West Asia," *Asian Survey*, Vol. 30, No. 9 (September 1990), pp. 862–876.

[12] John H. Lorentz, *The A to Z of Iran* (Lanham, MD: Scarecrow Press, 2007), pp. 119–121.

the several perplexing topics the country was juggling with. The East was supposed to be just a partner, not to say a junior partner, in the company of a loose coalition which the Khatami-led Iranian government invited to its sensational project of a "dialogue among civilizations." What particularly made the looking-East orientation still relevant during this period, even if unofficially, was Iran's pattern of international trade which was shifting in favor of more exchanges with China and other East Asian countries, especially South Korea.[13]

Meanwhile, what compelled Iran to soon revisit its looking-East approach, and even shore it up as a pillar of its official foreign policy, was the international controversy about the country's nuclear program. This clouded the final years of the Khatami government and, even more, the entire presidency of his dyed-in-the-wool populist successor, Mahmoud Ahmadinejad, whose reckless foreign policy backed Tehran into a calamitous corner without any clear diplomatic off-ramp in sight. This time, looking East was to display its promise simultaneously in all politico-strategic as well as in economic, technological, and cultural domains. Politically, Iran had to increasingly tilt toward the East in order to overcome its growing international isolation and neutralize a slew of multi-pronged sanctions levied against Tehran in the wake of its nuclear program.[14] With regard to the economic and technological aspects, the looking-East policy under the impulsive government of Ahmadinejad was to curry favor with many hard-charging corporations and investors from East Asia so that they could meet the country's growing demand. Moreover, the cultural element of the looking-East orientation was promoted by Tehran to primarily pave the ground for the desired outcomes of the economic and technological facets, leading to an unprecedented encroachment of East Asian countries upon the Iranian society in all those areas.[15]

When Hassan Rouhani was elected as Ahmadinejad's successor in June 2013, however, Iran's relations with the outside world unexpectedly underwent a seismic change. More importantly, the U.S.-led West's willingness to negotiate with the new Iranian government over the nuclear stalemate for a surprisingly prolonged period of eighteen months brought about significant developments in Tehran's foreign interactions. In particular, the ensuing results put the Iranian looking-East orientation in serious jeopardy

---

[13] Nathan Gonzalez, *Engaging Iran: The Rise of a Middle East Powerhouse and America's Strategic Choice* (Westport, CT: Praeger, 2007), pp. 99–101.

[14] Marc Lanteigne, *Chinese Foreign Policy: An Introduction*, third edition (Abingdon and New York: Routledge, 2016), p. 202.

[15] Shirzad Azad, *Iran and China: A New Approach to Their Bilateral Relations* (Lanham, MD: Lexington Books, 2017), pp. 63–64.

as some influential people in the country dared to even question the ratio-nale behind the policy in the first place.[16] In fact, a state of euphoria over a high possibility of rapprochement between Iran and the West that followed the signing of the Joint Comprehensive Plan of Action (JCPOA) between the Iranians and their counterparts in the Sextet (United Sates, France, Russia, Britain, Germany, and China) gave the sceptics a golden opportunity in order to challenge almost every aspect of the looking-East approach. By finger-wagging complaints and kvetching over specific cases of exploitation and abusive treatment of Iran by East Asian countries in the pre-JCPOA era, the opponents of looking East intended to particularly prepare the public opinion for a potential shift in the Iranian grand strategy away from the East and in favor of the West.[17]

Looking-East in Iran, however, proved once again to be both deep-rooted and resilient as the second term of the Rouhani presidency roughly coin-cided with the ascendancy of Donald Trump at the helm of American poli-tics. In sharp contrast to the approach of the Obama administration toward Iran, Trump tossed aside unilaterally the nuclear deal and then vowed to punish the country with "the most biting sanctions ever imposed."[18] More-over, Europe with which the Iranian government had developed better ties since 2013 was not in a strong position to either resist the Trump adminis-tration's anti-Iran policies thoroughly or provide Tehran with enough guar-anteed support in politico-economic and technological fields. The whole episode left the anti-looking-East forces in Iran in a very defensive position as the country was once again on the whims of its major partners in the East to survive the new bouts of international isolation and crippling economic sanctions.[19] Political inclinations and practical imperatives in Iran had been dubiously destined to be at odds for the umpteenth times, enabling the looking-East phoenix to pull through and, *sotto voce*, reap the reward.

---

[16] "Khanjarhay ashna: Safir pishin Iran dar sazeman melal be 'Kharidaar' migooyad chin, rusiyeh va hend ghabel etemad nistand" [Familiar Daggers: Iran's Ex-Ambassador to UN Tells 'Kharidaar' China, Russia and India are not Trustworthy], *Kharidaar*, July 11, 2018, p. 1.

[17] "Koreye jenoobi negaran chinishodan bazaar Iran" [South Korea Worried about Chinization of Iran Market], *Tabnak*, January 24, 2016; Azad, pp. 56, 61, 65; and "Khyanat be Iran, in bar tavassot chin!" [Betrayal of Iran, this Time by China!], *Kelid Daily*, May 20, 2018, pp. 1, 4.

[18] "Trump: Iran Sanctions Are 'Most Biting' Ever Imposed," *New York Post*, August 7, 2018; and "Donald Trump Says He Wants to Make Iran and North Korea Rich," *Newsweek*, August 26, 2019.

[19] "Gardesh be shargh" [Turn to East], *Farheekhtegan*, May 22, 2018, p. 9; and "Chiniha az tahrim Iran sood mibarand" [Chinese Benefit from Iran Sanctions], *Ghanoon Daily*, July 26, 2018, p. 3.

The military component: Once the meat, now just the gravy

Arms deals, and generally military affairs, greatly contributed to the initiation of a serious policy of looking East in Iran after the inception of the Islamic Republic and the follow-up Iran–Iraq War. It was actually this area of cooperation that sowed the seeds of instant cooperation between the new Iranian authorities and their counterparts in China and North Korea, though South Korea and Taiwan also engaged in some limited yet stealthy deals in armaments with Tehran during the war.[20] Besides that critical initial impact, the military component played an important role in the continuation of the Iranian looking-East approach in the aftermath of the Iran–Iraq War. In fact, military and defense cooperation endured, *mutatis mutandis*, to serve as a pillar of Iran's foreign policies toward East Asian countries no matter if only China and North Korea in the region were relevant to this sensitive business. And while the military element persisted in being consequential in the official ties between Iran and China, it remained the *raison d'être* of bilateral relationship between Tehran and Pyongyang in long run.

Moreover, the military component became a touchstone whereby many other stakeholders could measure the Iranian looking-East policy and its ramifications on Tehran's connections to East Asia. It was the very military cooperation between Iran and East Asia which, from the beginning, made the whole concept of looking-East approach highly sensitive. Short of delicate deals in arms and military equipment between Tehran and the East Asian states, i.e. China and North Korea, there were hardly any compelling rationale for many other parties here and there to put the entire relationship of Tehran with that region on notice right after the outbreak of the Iran–Iraq War.[21] It was again for this pivotal reason that Iran's subsequent ties to its partners in East Asia became a subject of tight scrutiny after the bloody war brought to an end in 1988.[22] Iran's post war-looking-East orientation certainly experienced a lot of dynamisms, but it was almost always the military ingredient which captured both the interest and attention of many other stakeholders.

---

[20] Michael Brzoska, "Profiteering on the Iran–Iraq War," *Bulletin of the Atomic Scientists*, June 1987, pp. 42–45.

[21] Patrick M. Cronin, ed., *Double Trouble: Iran and North Korea as Challenges to International Security* (Westport, CT: Praeger Security International, 2008).

[22] Michael Eisenstadt, "Chinese Military Assistance to Iran: An Overview," in Benjamin A. Gilman, ed., *Consequences of China's Military Sales to Iran: Hearing Before the Committee on International Relations, House of Representatives*, One Hundred Fourth Congress, second session, September 12, 1996 (Washington, D.C.: U.S. Government Printing Office, 1996), pp. 37–40.

On top of that, Iran's military and defense interactions with East Asia became a bone of contention between the advocates and critics of the looking-East orientation. Of course, the line between the two groups was pretty much blurred during the Iran–Iraq War period when there was little, if any, difference across the political spectrum with regard to securing the war requirements in every possible way. In the post-war era, however, the dividing line between the proponents and opponents of military connections to East Asia began to give way to an open yet cautious avowal of differences. Supporters particularly gave prominence to the timely and constructive role of East Asian countries to meet Iran's urgent military needs during the war with Iraq. In their view, moreover, the war-time's unique contribution of East Asia needed to be regarded as a blueprint for any future cooperation in military and defense affairs between the two parties simply because those Asian states had already proved that they could be helpful and reliable for Tehran in tough times.[23]

Meanwhile, the critics of military and defense interactions with East Asia were not all liberal and pro-West forces as this group also included isolationists and nativists whose considerations and priorities in foreign policy were contrasting, though their reservation about and objection to close military cooperation with the East happened to be less vocal and less hard-hitting. The critics primarily worried that purchasing more and more military stuff of subpar quality from East Asian countries could potentially put at risk the capabilities and readiness of Iran's armed forces in long haul. They emphasized their point by, for instance, highlighting the growing investment by some of Iran's neighbors in more sophisticated defense and military equipment. These goods were supplied through the Western countries and were based on newfangled technologies. Additionally, the critics had other, more immediate concerns, as they did not want the West to put the spotlight on Iran because of the country's "suspicious" military and missile cooperation with East Asian countries.[24]

Regardless of all those contrasting views, looking East in military affairs in Iran moved pretty much in synch with the politico-diplomatic dynamics. As exemplified by its politico-ideological slogans, the Islamic Republic initially and self-righteously rejected to buy arms from the Soviet Union, while it soon purchased almost any type of Soviet-made weapons from North Korea, China, Libya, and a number of Eastern European countries. During the Iran–Iraq War period, arms purchases from North Korea and China were

---

[23] "Gardesh be shargh" [Turn to East], *Farheekhtegan*, May 22, 2018, pp. 1, 9.
[24] "Raz bazi ba barg shargh" [Secret of Playing with Eastern Card], *Kharidaar*, June 24, 2018, p. 1.

particularly very critical as Pyongyang and Beijing supplied about 43 percent of the imported weapons in 1985, and almost 70 percent a year later.[25] This was in sharp contrast to the pattern of looking West in arms which Iran had experienced roughly a decade earlier. As a case in point, Iran had purchased some 77 percent of its armaments from the United States worth more than $7 billion between 1972 and 1977 alone, making even the Western European countries queasy because Washington was then selling more and quality weapons to Tehran than it was selling to any other ally including Israel.[26]

In the post war era, arms purchases from East Asia lost its significance over time as cooperation with the region in non-military affairs gradually became a major characteristic of the Iranian looking-East approach. Still, the Iranian–North Korean connections continued, for quite long, to remain as a highly contentious aspect of the looking-East orientation because the cooperation between the two countries now involved some critical missile and probably nuclear issues. Iran's military cooperation with China, however, underwent new dynamism as Beijing was walking on eggshells trying to give priority to its rising interests in the West.[27] As a corollary to that, China either terminated or highly regulated its military and missile deals with Iran in order to draw less attention to an over increasing level of interactions between the two countries in other areas. In recent years, Iran and China have once again vowed to expand and deepen their military and defense connections part of which might come into being as an implication of the Chinese "One Belt, One Road" initiative, but little has really been detailed on the broad nature and scope of such prospective collaborations between the two sides.[28]

Technology transfer: On the coattails of politics

As experienced by all newly-industrialized nations, the transfer of advanced technology can speed up amply the process of growth and economic development. Technical know-how is also a key force to sustain the industrial power and economic strength of a country.[29] A serious policy

---

[25] Anthony H. Cordesman, *The Iran–Iraq War and Western Security, 1984–1987: Strategic Implications and Policy Options* (London: Jane's Publishing, 1987), p. 29.

[26] Adam Tarock, *The Superpowers' Involvement in the Iran–Iraq War* (Commack, NY: Nova Science Publishers, 1998), pp. 73, 93.

[27] "Zhonggong 'pengyou quan' buduan kuoda" [The Chinese Communist Party's 'Circle of Friends' Keeps Expanding], *Renmin*, December 12, 2017.

[28] For more information on Iran's role in China's OBOR initiative, see: Feng Bing, 'Yidai yilu': *Quanqiu fazhande zhongguo luoji* ['One Belt, One Road': The Chinese Logic for Global Development] (Beijing: Zhongguo minzhu fazhi chubanshe, 2015).

[29] Allan C. Reddy, *A Macro Perspective on Technology Transfer* (Westport, Connecticut and London: Quorum Books, 1996), pp. 4–5; and Howard Pack, "Asian Successes vs. Middle

of technology transfer has, therefore, a long history in Iran, harkening back at least to the post-oil shock of 1973 when the country, under the Pahlavi monarchy, vowed to join the ranks of the world's industrialized countries by the end of the twentieth century.[30] Besides exhausting potential in the West, Iran even turned to East Asia for exploring new ways of transferring technical expertise and industrial knowledge. Two cases of such technology quest were, for instance, the signing of the $3.6 billion industrial project of Iran–Japan Petrochemical Complex (IJPC) with the Japanese Mitsui and the 50-50 joint refining venture between the National Iranian Oil Corporation (NIOC) and the South Korea Ssangyang Corporation. Both projects eventually failed, and this early technological looking-East adventure thereby went into tailspin after the Pahlavi dynasty reluctantly passed the torch.[31]

Under the Islamic Republic, technology transfer was not a first priority of the government, as the country was grappling with urgent war requirements throughout the 1980–1988 period. In the post-war era, reconstruction and development programs as well as increasing industrial and economic demand forced the successive Iranian governments to delve into all possible methods for bringing in the required technology and industrial skills. Since Iran's relationship with the West remained frosty, one decade after another, the transfer of technology needed to gradually emerge as a major aspect of the looking-East orientation. Still, the technological looking-East policy hardly achieved a major breakthrough under any reformist or conservative government as the policy itself was constantly encountering a number of critical internal and extern impediments. Internally, technology transfer, like some other areas, was burdened with malaises such as unstable exchange rates, mismanagement of foreign exchange, and an unsound economic structure exemplified by a dominant influence of the state in almost all politico-economic decision-making processes, though the private sector was often encouraged to play a more visible role.[32]

Externally, looking East for technology, like all other steps and methods taken to acquire technology somewhere else, was quite overshadowed by Iran's political, and especially nuclear and missile, stalemates with the West. The country was perpetually suspected that it was using the imported tech-

Eastern Failures: The Role of Technology Transfer in Economic Development," *Issues in Science and Technology*, Vol. 24, No. 3 (Spring 2008), pp. 47–54.

[30] Robert Graham, *Iran: The Illusion of Power* (New York: St. Martin's Press, 1978), pp. 113, 206.

[31] The Financial Times, *Financial Times Oil and Gas International Year Book* (London: Longman, 1983), p. 481.

[32] Goel Cohen, *Technology Transfer: Strategic Management in Developing Countries* (London: Sage Publications, 2004), p. 195; and "People vs. Dinosaurs," *The New York Times*, June 8, 2008, p. WK12.

nologies to fast-track its nuclear and missile programs. Such accusations were especially piercing with regard to the dual-use and sensitive technologies which could be easily manipulated for military and nuclear projects. Allegations of such genre naturally paved the way for new and more severe regimes of sanctions levied again Iran, aiming to curtail the country's ability to have convenient access to foreign technologies and industrial know-how. Of course, even East Asian countries were not really willing to share with Iran, on a silver platter, their latest technologies and sensitive technical knowledge regardless of how the country was going to use them. But the sanctions had the power to seriously curtail their level and scope of technological cooperation with Iran in many other safe and routine fields on a selective and limited basis.

An overwhelming majority of Iran's foreign partners for technology transfer in both public and private sectors, therefore, succumbed ineluctably to incessant arm-twisting strategies of the United States that emerged virtually as the main architect behind carving out and implementing several types of sanctions against the Iranians since November 1979. Exerting pressure upon the American friends and allies often proved to be an easy task, while Washington could sometimes resort to any tool in its disposal in order to convince, or even compel, US rivals and adversaries not to help Iran with technology and industrial know-how.[33] The meat of the matter was that the US government developed, over time, a series of legal measures to wield tremendous pressure on foreign entities which were willing to engage in transferring certain types of technologies to Iran. Those legal tools made it quite possible for Washington to inflict a hefty penalty on targeted foreign entities "by freezing their US properties, limiting their ability to trade with the United States, prohibiting them from obtaining US government procurement contracts, or otherwise impairing their ability to work with US entities."[34]

In the face of all those hurdles and setbacks, the Iranian looking-East approach needed to take care of the country's growing technological requirements, even by unconventional means if required. As the first and second steel and petrochemicals producer in the Middle East, respectively, for instance, Iran and its expanding consumer constituency of some 80 million people perpetually required to import — lock, stock, and barrel — advanced

---

[33] Christopher M. Blanchard and Paul K. Kerr, *United Arab Emirates Nuclear Program and Proposed U.S. Nuclear Cooperation*, CRS Report for Congress, December 23, 2009 (Washington, D.C.: Congressional Research Service, 2009), p. 11.

[34] United States Government Accountability Office (USGAO), *Iran Sanctions: Complete and Timely Licensing Data Needed to Strengthen Enforcement of Export Restrictions*, Report to Congressional Requesters, March 2010 (Washington, D.C.: USGAO, 2010), p. 24.

technical and industrial goods. Obliging its East Asian conventional partners to share technology and invest in industrial knowhow gradually became a semi-official policy of the Iranian government, enabling it to use the acquired foreign technologies to satisfy the insatiable domestic demands and improving the country's rising export potential.[35] For large and resourceful Eastern companies, establishing joint ventures with major Iranian companies was sometimes a fitting formula, while large financial rewards could occasionally temp smaller East Asian firms, and even private Asian businessmen or businesswomen with the dual nationality of a Western country, to sneakily supply to Iran this or other desired type of technology, and if necessary its old or obsolete version.

Crude oil: The lubricating fluid of looking East

Unlike other aspects of the looking-East approach which involved an Iranian initiative, oil certainly played a major role in persuading East Asian states to themselves make overtures to Iran from the 1950s onward. Iran for long time remained either the most important or a major supplier of crude oil to Japan, South Korea and Taiwan, while the Iranian government under the Pahlavi monarchy replied back the well-intention of its East Asian customers by refusing to boycott them in the wake of the 1973 crisis during which the Arab countries of the Middle East had decided to stop supplying oil to all US allies here and there.[36] Oil even played a part in the pre-Islamic Republic chapter of North Korea's relationship with Iran to such an extent that Pyongyang negotiated in March 1975 a $200 million loan from Tehran in order to cover shipments of Iranian crude oil. In the same way, the Maoist Chinese started to purchase small quantities of Iranian oil after 1974 when China itself was still an exporter of petroleum before becoming a net importer of oil some two decades later.[37]

Under the Islamic Republic, oil still remained a pivotal factor in the strategic thinking of almost all East Asian states toward Iran. They desperately needed the Iranian crude oil no matter what type of political system or ideological doctrine was ruling the country. The oil dependency of East Asian states thus facilitated the ground for the Iranian officials to forge friendly ties with their Asian counterparts, bankrolling Tehran's critical policies toward

---

[35] Robert J. Shapiro, *Futurecast: How Superpowers, Populations, and Globalization Will Change Your World by the Year 2020* (New York: St. Martin's Griffin, 2009), pp. 274–275.

[36] Leon Howell and Michael Morrow, *Asia, Oil Politics and the Energy Crisis: The Haves and the Have-nots* (New York: International Documentation, 1974), p. 51.

[37] Robert Slater, *Seizing Power: The Grab for Global Oil Wealth* (Hoboken, NJ: John Wiley & Sons, 2010), p. 29.

the region, especially its nascent looking-East orientation. As oil gradually made up a lion's share of Iran's exports to several East Asian countries, and as oil revenues accounted for a great part of the Iranian government's annual national budget one year after another, however, the petroleum pendulum slowly but surely swung in the other direction to favor East Asia. The looking-East approach was to be ineluctably affected by this new development because from now on the policy orientation had to strive, in every possible way, to assure a safe and sufficient amount of oil supply to Iran's East Asian partners.[38]

Of course, the emergence of new petroleum suppliers from different parts of the world and the ensuing glut of cheap oil on the markets played a critical role in curtailing the erstwhile desperate of East Asia for the Iranian crude. The situation aggravated virtually from the time the United States-drafted a slew of biting economic sanctions effectively targeted Iran's oil exports. This happened surprisingly under the Obama administration, but his successor, Trump, also found the crude export a powerful weapon for browbeating Tehran. Consequently, the country was forced to sell oil only to a small number of countries most of which located in Asia, while fewer countries among that remaining coterie were in a comfortable position to import a large share of the Iranian crude. The plight was aggravated when, under certain sanctions regulations and diktats, Iran could no longer receive its oil money from those few countries which possessed an American permission (like South Korea) or enjoyed some international clout (like China) to continue buying the Iranian crude.[39]

The US-led pressures on Iran's oil exports and energy revenues, the country's largest source of foreign exchange, certainly created problems for the project of Looking East. Prior to Trump's oil threat against Tehran, China, South Korea and Japan were importing some 27, 10 and 7 percent of Iran's crude oil exports, respectively. Even without counting the oil which Iran was supplying to Taiwan and North Korea, close to half of the Iranian petroleum exports were flowing to East Asia, making the region a very important strategic partner as the country needed these revenues in order to manage its day-to-day affairs.[40] As stated clearly by their authorities, Iran's East Asian oil customers were no longer desperate for the Iranian oil because there were

---

[38] "Frestadegan Iran dar gharb va shargh" [Iranian Envoys in West and East], *Hamshahri*, July 12, 2018, pp. 1, 3.

[39] "Koreye jenoobi varedat naft az Iran ra be toor kamel motavagghef kard" [South Korea Completely Suspended Importing Iran Oil], *Abrar Eghtesadi*, September 24, 2018, p. 1.

[40] Michael L. Ross, *The Oil Curse: How Petroleum Wealth Shapes the Development of Nations* (Princeton and Oxford: Princeton University Press, 2012), pp. 7-8.

other oil producers waiting to supply more than enough crude to the region.[41] Although countries like China were not willing, for strategic and economic reasons, to quit importing Iranian oil altogether, they were expecting to be given some extra bonus under such special circumstances befallen Iran.[42]

It was, therefore, reported that Iran offered discounted oil in an attempt to curry favor with its crude customers in East Asia and somewhere else. Moreover, Iran had apparently proposed preferential investment opportunities to its oil partners in exchange for continuous oil purchases at desired quantities, though the authorities in Tehran considered such sensational measures to be quite normal in international energy markets. On top of that, Iran's over dependence on its East Asia for crude exports and oil incomes was to tip the scales handsomely in favor of its Asian partners, giving them out of the blue significant leverage over the country's political economy as a whole.[43] This somber situation would also deal a devastating blow to the whole concept of looking East, turning it into virtually the only option left for the Iranian government in coping with an unsympathetic world.

Importing goods: On the lookout to substitute

A common element in the looking-East approach was to purchase all sorts of non-military goods from East Asian states and to use the practice as a bargaining chip in dealing with those countries. This was not difficult; moreover, certain policies of East Asian countries amply facilitated this Iranian undertaking in the region. From the first oil shock of 1973 onward, recycling part of the oil revenues earned by Middle Eastern countries, Iran in particular, became a high priority of the export-oriented policies in the developing and industrializing East Asia.[44] Furthermore, the other critically important incentive was to bring down an expanding trade deficit with the Middle East because of additional imports of energy resources from the region. Japan, Taiwan, South Korea, and later China all drew a bead on insatiable and bankable markets of Iran, carving out different strategies at different stages of their economic growth in order to increase their exports to Iran, though this staunch orientation was equally persuaded in some other parts

---

[41] "Who Actually Benefits from Sanctions on Iran?" *Russia Today*, July 19, 2018.

[42] "Sorry, Iran, China isn't Going to Save You," *Bloomberg*, June 27, 2018; and "US Oil Sanction Threat won't Shake China's Energy Sector: Observer," *Global Times*, July 2, 2018.

[43] "Iran Makes Hard Turn East as Fate of Nuclear Deal Dims," *Al Jazeera*, June 8, 2018.

[44] John W. Limbert, *Iran: At War with History* (Boulder, CO: Westview Press, 1987), pp. 14–16.

of the world simply because of the export-oriented nature of development model in East Asia.[45]

Although Tehran trades virtually with every country in the world, there happened to be equally good reasons for many of Iran's domestic markets to succumb over time to almost every type of manufactured products supplied by East Asia. Relative geographic proximity, lower costs of imports, a greater flow of Iranian oil toward the East, and a policy of importing low-cost products to satisfy citizens in the middle- to lower-income brackets each certainly played an important role in accelerating the rate and scope of imports from East Asia. Iran's chilly relationship with the West and especially the intensifying regime of sanctions levied against Tehran, however, tremendously influenced the dynamics of imports into Iran from East Asian countries over the past several decades.[46] The looking-East approach was thereby tasked with a key objective of sorting out domestic requirements by importing all kinds of commodities which the Iranians were no longer able to purchase from the West because of the sanctions diktats.

As a corollary to that, for instance, a seismic regional shift took place in the Iranian pattern of imports between 1994 and 2006; the share of the European Union declined markedly from more than 50 percent to around one-third, while the share of Asia ratcheted up from 9 to 27 percent.[47] After 2006, the East Asian countries of South Korea and China particularly dominated Iran's imports from Asia as some brands from these two Eastern countries successfully made inroads into almost every Iranian household. Some European countries like Germany could occasionally, especially in the halcyon period between the signing of the JCPOA and the withdrawal from the nuclear deal by the Trump administration, increase their share of exports into Iran, but the European bloc as a whole never managed to claim back its erstwhile dominant position in the Persian Gulf country. In sharp contrast to a number of Western nations such as the Germans, the Chinese made perennially significant progress in lucrative Iranian markets by positioning themselves as the largest imports partner of Iran, accounting for roughly one-fourth of the country's imported goods.

According to the latest data, China, the United Arab Emirates, and South Korea occupy the position of the top three imports partners for Iran, supplying 24.62, 14.67, and 7.92 percent of the country's total imports,

---

[45] Dwight H. Perkins, *East Asian Development: Foundations and Strategies* (Cambridge, MA: Harvard University Press, 2013).

[46] Denny Roy, *Return of the Dragon: Rising China and Regional Security* (New York: Columbia University Press, 2013), pp. 172–175.

[47] United States Government Accountability Office, *Iran Sanctions: Impact Good or Bad?* (New York: Nova Science Publishers, 2008), p. 29.

respectively.[48] Of course, the UAE does not have any credible brand of its own, and a great deal of what it exports are products it receives from others, Western and particularly Eastern countries, before the tiny Arab state re-exports them to profitable final destinations such as Iran. In 2017, for instance, exports and re-exports to Iran from the UAE reached more than $17 billion, mostly through the entrepôt of Dubai.[49] The foregoing figures, however, usually do not cover the majority of East Asian products which are constantly being smuggled and imported informally into Iran through a slew of porous borders surrounding Iran. This phenomenon also contributed profoundly to the omnipresence of East Asian brands and goods throughout the Iranian society sometimes with critical ramifications for Iran's ties to the region, and generally its looking-East orientation.

The crux of the problem was that imports became so profitable that many people went into the business, giving rise to the destruction of domestic brands and products, a massive shutdown of companies, and large lay-offs.[50] Many citizens were further agitated because of the low quality of the goods imported, particularly from China, just at a time when people were already upset at the perceived response of East Asian countries to the West-led sanctions. The public was expecting the looking-East policy to cushion such jolts. As a consequence of all these disagreeable developments and lamentable experiences, many among the intellectuals and educated echelons eventually joined the crowd of looking-East sceptics, questioning the rationale behind the Iranian government's insistence on forging closer connections to East Asian countries without convincing its constituency that how the Iranian society in general was to benefit from such relations on an equal footing in long run.[51]

Diversification: Bringing variety to non-oil exports

The vision for generating non-oil revenues to be on a par with the income Iran makes from exporting crude oil essentially harkens back to the pre-first oil shock era. The very first oil shock actually dealt a severe blow to the dream of having a dynamic non-oil economy with kinetic energy for

---

[48] Data is taken from the official website of the Islamic Republic of Iran Customs Administration (IRICA) available at http:// www.irica.gov.ir.

[49] "US Sanctions on Iran Affect Trade with UAE," *Financial Tribune*, August 15, 2018.

[50] "Hame mikhahand varedkonandeh shavand" [Everyone Wants to Become Importer], *Vatan-e Emrooz*, June 23, 2018, pp. 1, 3.

[51] "Be chiniha zyad chelo kebab nadahid!" [Do not Give Chinese too much Chelo Kebab!], *Aftab-e Yazd*, May 24, 2018, p. 1; and "Barkhord doganeh sharghiha, tardid sherkathay gharbi" [Double-dealing of Easterners, Dubiousness of Western Companies], *Hamshahri*, June 2, 2018, pp. 5, 6.

exports and self-sustainability as the country was swiftly swept into an orgy of spending, consumerism, and indulgence. In the aftermath of the second oil shock, moreover, the thought of having a national budget markedly independent of oil earnings became further untenable because Iran subsequently encountered a humongous hemorrhage of human, financial, and natural resources, all of which strategically required to build a robust, competitive, and enterprising economy. The follow-up Iran–Iraq War was another bout that wreaked havoc on Iran's domestic production and non-oil exports, compelling the country to mobilize all of its domestic resources in order to survive the tumultuous conditions of an eight-year long military campaign dubbed the longest conventional conflict of the twentieth century.[52]

After the end of the Iran–Iraq War and the commencement of reconstruction programs, assisting the non-oil sectors of the Iranian economy and increasing the share of non-energy exports once again became an important plan of the government; a policy which was to be later endorsed and often promoted equally by successive conservative and reformist governments. One critical reason behind this strategy was the frequent fluctuation in oil prices, which could sometimes become a major setback for the estimated national budget and a hazardous hiccup in funding the planned reconstruction and development programs.[53] More importantly, the continuation of frosty politico-diplomatic relationship with the West as well as the repercussions of different sanctions imposed on Iran badly influenced the overall situation of the Iranian economy, forcing the government to find alternatives ways, such as the promotion of non-oil exports as a means of earning foreign exchange, in order to gain some stability in financial and monetary policies.[54]

As part of the looking-East orientation, therefore, Iran paid particular attention to East Asian markets for its growing volume of non-crude oil exports. Of course, domestic markets in Japan, South Korea, and Taiwan were not traditionally in favor of purchasing more non-oil products from Iran, but even importers from these countries, South Koreans in particular, were convinced to gradually increase their share of Iranian products besides crude oil. Another far more favorable target in the region was China, whose domestic consumer markets were expanding by leaps and bounds one year after another. This whetted the appetite of many Iranians in both the public and private sectors to capitalize on prospective Chinese demand for

---

[52] Fred M. Shelley, *The World's Population: An Encyclopedia of Critical Issues, Crises, and Ever-Growing Countries* (Santa Barbara, CA: ABC-CLIO, 2015), pp. 255–257.

[53] Robert McNally, *Crude Volatility: The History and the Future of Boom-Bust Oil Prices* (New York: Columbia University Press, 2017), pp. 139–141.

[54] Kenneth Katzman, *The Persian Gulf States: Post-War Issues* (New York: Novinka Books, 2004), pp. 5–6.

Iran's non-oil exports. This upbeat outlook about China coincided with the dwindling potential of markets in the West, which had long been the main destination for Iran's traditional and famous non-oil products. The ongoing regime of crippling economic sanctions had also played a very effective role in ruining market access in the West.[55]

The looking-East approach was partially successful in catapulting Iranian non-oil products into East Asian markets, making China and South Korea into two of Iran's top five destinations for non-crude oil exports. China eventually became the largest customer for Iranian non-oil goods, importing products ranging from marble to minerals and from pistachios to petrochemicals. In recent years, China's share of the country's non-oil products has been on the increase, and so has China's clout over the Iranian international trade, importing something around 19–25 percent annually; a figure interestingly pretty close to what Iran imports from that East Asian country each year.

Moreover, the UAE has again played a dubious role in laying the ground for the promotion of Iranian non-oil exports, as the Arab country is now one of the top three destinations for Iran's non-energy goods. Some of the non-oil products which Iran supply to the UAE would ultimately find their way into the bustling consumer markets of East Asia after being repackaged and re-exported.[56]

Meanwhile, the resolve of the looking-East policy to ship larger cargos of non-oil goods to East Asia was not really without disapproval and defiance in Iran. Exporting non-oil Iranian products to other parts of the world was certainly a safe and less contentious issue as juxtaposed against a disputable and often ill-advised practice of flooding domestic markets with any type of foreign goods. Still, cherry-picking and hoarding certain desirable goods and then selling them to other countries, often managed by a number of unscrupulous monopolies, had far-reaching ramifications for the society in large.[57] This was particularly the case when a sharp plummet in the value of the national currency could make it hard for many middle- to lower-income families to buy exportable exotic products — access to and purchase of which they had long taken for granted. It was simply unacceptable and outrageous for such a susceptible group of citizens when they had to bargain over imported saffron and walnuts of subpar quality, while similar stuff of

[55] "Tahrimha miravand, chin nemiravad" [Sanctions will Disappear, China will Hold on], *Ghanoon Daily*, April 8, 2015, p. 8.

[56] International Monetary Fund, *United Arab Emirates: 2011 Article IV Consultation — Staff Report* (Washington, D.C.: International Monetary Fund, 2011), pp. 12–13.

[57] "Sood varedat 200 darsad, sood toolid haddaksar 20 darsad!" [Imports Pay off 200 Percent, Production Pays off no More than 20 Percent!], *Kayhan*, May 28, 2018, pp. 1, 4.

much higher quality and reputation, produced in Iran, became inaccessible to them due to their being exported wholesale to China and other countries.[58]

Cultural links: Belated overtures

In the realm of culture, there has been less looking East than in other areas of bilateral interactions. In fact, Iran's cultural interests turned out to be focused mostly on its own immediate region as well as on the legendary West, whose introduction to popular socio-political discourse in the society since the nineteen century preoccupied many Iranians across the political spectrum, one generation after another. Moreover, East Asian societies themselves encountered a similar phenomenon which had a profound impact on their cultural connections to some other regions, including the Middle East. As a corollary to that, when Iran established formal politico-diplomatic ties with East Asian countries in modern times, culture — and cultural affairs generally — hardly became a very hot issue or a contentious topic involving the two sides, though they often signed a raft of cultural agreements and engaged in many cultural programs and events.[59]

Iran under Pahlavi, for instance, used to have close relationship with Japan, South Korea, and Taiwan until 1971 when Tehran switched its diplomatic allegiance from Taipei to Beijing. From holding friendly soccer match to giving approval to town twinning, Iran certainly engaged in many cultural activities with the region over years. But such cultural undertakings were predominantly about some strategic and politico-economic considerations rather than about any genuine cultural attachment to East Asian countries. Even when the Shah vowed to create a "second Japan" in the Middle East, his hypothetical vision was ultimately about accomplishing certain economic and technological objectives by Iran.[60] For all the cultural contributions to the successful rise of Japan in the aftermath of World War II and despite so many critical developments unfolding in other East Asian countries during his reign, the Shah visited Japan and Taiwan only once in June 1958, while the political capitals of many Western countries became his royal rendezvous until he was removed from power in early 1979.[61]

---

[58] "Lavazem khanegi irani ghorbani mafiaye varedkonandeh" [Iranian Furniture Victim of Imports Mafia] *Jahan Sanat*, June 19, 2016, p. 12; and "Sanat kafsh Iran zire paye varedat" [Iran's Footwear Industry Steamrolled by Imports], *Farheekhtegan*, May 21, 2018, p. 9.

[59] "Iran Turns East: A Chronology of Iranian Relations with the Eastern Bloc and China," *Middle East Economic Digest (MEED)*, July 10, 1989, p. 3.

[60] Andrew S. Cooper, *The Oil Kings: How the U.S., Iran, and Saudi Arabia Changed the Balance of Power in the Middle East* (New York: Simon & Schuster Paperbacks, 2011), p. 21.

[61] James A. Bill, *The Eagle and the Lion: The Tragedy of American–Iranian Relations* (New Haven and London: Yale University Press, 1988), p. 154.

When the Islamic Republic came to power, Iran initially became more alienated from East Asia culturally. The "neither the East, nor the West" motto left no doubt that the new socio-political culture emerged in Iran could hardly be captivated by the communist culture of China and North Korea, while the American allies of Japan and South Korea were in a less favorable position to win over Tehran in terms of the new cultural lexicon championed by many top authorities of the Islamic Republic.[62] After all, East Asia was far away, and the countries located in that region were not perceived to be a fertile ground for the ardent promotion of the political ideology the Islamic Republic stood for.[63] During the ensuing Iran–Iraq War period, culture mattered little in Tehran's growing politico-military connections to East Asia; hard politics dominated everything and genuine people to people interactions between Iranians and their counterparts in the region were almost non-existent.

In the aftermath of the Iran–Iraq War, culture did gradually and sporadically play a part in areas of interactions involving Iran and its East Asian partners. A number of historical Japanese and Chinese dramas were dubbed and broadcast through national TV channels before the arrival of the Korean Wave (Hallyu) about one and half decades later. Moreover, East Asian countries were invited to participate in cultural programs which were initiated and hosted by Tehran, here and there, under the "dialogue among civilizations" project during the presidency of Khatami. Despite their immediate importance, developments of this genre eventually proved to be ephemeral, producing little tangible results in the long-term with regard to bridging the existing cultural gaps between Iran and East Asia societies.[64] These so-called cultural measures were launched to primarily serve immediate political and economic interests instead of making a permanent contribution to Iranian-East Asian cultural dynamics.

In spite of the impediments and limitations, however, over the past 15 or so years the Iranian looking-East approach has apparently accorded culture a more significant role in hopes of materializing critical objectives in East Asia in the long run. In fact, from the commencement of the Ahmadinejad presidency onward, the role of culture has been more discernible in Iran's

[62] "Negah be shargh va asl na sharghi va na gharbi" [Looking-East and the Principle of Neither East Nor West], *Javan*, September 15, 2018, p. 1.

[63] Gary J. Schmitt, ed., *Rise of the Revisionists: Russia, China, and Iran* (Washington, D.C.: American Enterprise Institute, 2018).

[64] Lu Jin and Zhang Liming, *Yilang: Dongxi fang wenming de huihe dian* [Iran: The Meeting Point of Eastern and Western Civilizations] (Hong Kong: Xianggang chengshi daxue chubanshe [City University of Hong Kong Press], 2011); and James A. Millward, *The Silk Road: A Very Short Introduction* (New York: Oxford University Press, 2013), pp. 49, 71

multifaceted connections to East Asian countries.[65] In politico-diplomatic circles as well as in business and scholarly meetings involving the two sides, reference to culture and cultural issues almost became an integral part of talks and discussions.[66] More importantly, Iran launched, albeit belatedly, academic studies about East Asian countries at a number of top universities, particularly those located in Tehran, and the country's major policy research institutes as well as think tanks paid more attention to East Asia. The looking-East orientation had long ignored the cultural facet, and such late measures were intended to partially make up for that drawback.[67]

Conclusion

Perhaps inadvertently and unwittingly, Iran embarked upon a policy of looking-East far ahead of the time when that became a prevailing trend in the world. The nature and scope of the Iranian move also differed in important ways from similar courses of action eventually taken by other nations. In fact, few others adopted a looking-East approach as diverse and multifaceted as Iran's. More importantly, the Iranian looking-East drive turned out to be a litmus test of sorts by which other stakeholders could conveniently, and often accurately, get the measure of Tehran's strategic plans and foreign policy attitudes toward a large part of the world. For Iran, the internal implications of the approach were equally, if not say more, salient regardless of the fact that looking-East was initially formulated, and later maintained and buttressed up, to meet certain domestic requirements in almost all politico-strategic, military, economic, technological and cultural areas.

In spite of its profound impacts, however, Iran's looking-East approach did not prove to be very well calculated. A fair number of the officials and advisers who played a key role in designing and implementing looking-East over the decades had other policy priorities in mind that outweighed the importance of steady and wide-ranging relations with East Asian countries. Additionally, "Looking East" was subordinate to the gyrations in Iran's relationship with the West, and it was often adjusted based on expediency. This meant that consistent attempts to address Iran's domestic imperatives by looking East were hard to achieve.

---

[65] Shirzad Azad, "Principalism Engages Pragmatism: Iran's Relations with East Asia under Ahmadinejad," *Asian Politics & Policy*, Vol. 7, No. 4 (October 2015), pp. 555–573.

[66] Henelito A. Sevilla, Jr., ed., *Philippine–Iran Relations: 50 Years and Beyond* (Quezon City, Philippines: Asian Center, University of the Philippines Diliman, 2017).

[67] "Charkhesh az bloc gharb be bloc shargh" [Shifting from Western Bloc to Eastern Bloc], *Shargh Daily*, April 4, 2018, p. 4.

The volatility of the West's relations with Iran thus created unsteady conditions in which to launch stable and reliable ties with the East. But soon the importance of an eastward focus for Iran's peace and prosperity has become starkly clear. If looking-East had sometimes seemed to be just an attractive alternative, from now on it was recognized as an acute necessity, with both domestic and international implications. Currently, the lion's share of the two-way trade between Iran and its eastern partners hinges on stable, symbiotic connections, which lend greater credibility to the strength and durability of the looking-East approach. Regardless of the predicted tectonic shifts in the relationship between Iran and the West, looking East will certainly endure as a linchpin of Iranian's approach to the outside world for the foreseeable future.

CHAPTER 2. SAUDI ARABIA: MAKING CONTINGENCY PLANS AMID ANXIETY

It is axiomatic for people in academic positions or in policy and media circles to see the Kingdom of Saudi Arabia as highly dependent, completely enmeshed in the U.S.-led alliance system. In fact, the Western orientation of the Saudis is emphasized so strongly that many observers find it hard to imagine that they might ever have contemplated taking a different approach.[68] According to this parsimonious interpretation of events, Saudi Arabia formulates its domestic and even its foreign and security priorities in compliance with Washington's plans and preferences; the top Saudi leadership would be highly unlikely to make any major move without U.S. approval, neither to breach its commitments nor to stray significantly from the pattern of regional and international partnerships outside the U.S-led coalition.[69]

Belying such beliefs, however, cautiously but practically, Saudi Arabia has edged into a new approach in its foreign policy over the past two decades. A fresh east wind has breathed new life into the kingdom's modest diplomatic efforts. In adopting a pro-East policy of sorts, the Saudis have not merely been sending up trial balloons; they have been both convinced and determined in this initiative.[70] This evolving orientation is not diametrically opposed the Saudis' traditional staunch attachment to the U.S.-led alli-

---

[68] Geoffrey Simons, *Saudi Arabia: The Shape of a Client Feudalism* (London: Macmillan, 1998), pp. 309–310.

[69] Stig Stenslie, "The End of Elite Unity and the Stability of Saudi Arabia," *The Washington Quarterly*, Vol. 41, No. 1 (2018), pp. 61–82.

[70] "Saudi Arabia Pursues a 'Look-East Policy'," *The New York Times*, January 26, 2006.

ance matrix, but the prospects and possible ramifications of Saudi Arabia's growing connections to the East seem to have broken the West's monopoly in Riyadh.[71] True, the Trump administration embraced a more pro-Saudi stance since assuming office in January 2017 as compared to Barack Obama, but it can never be taken for granted that the next American president, no matter Democrat or Republican, will stick to Trump's approach to Saudi Arabia.

Why, then, did the Saudis decide to adopt a looking-East orientation in the first place? Could the new policy be an American stratagem instead of Saudi Arabia's own long-overdue initiative? Was some third party instrumental in convincing them that such a shift was inevitable? To what extent did the Looking-east policy of the Arab kingdom diverge from Riyadh's long-lasting reliance on and loyalty to the United States and certain other major Western powers? Moreover, what is the real nature of Saudi Arabia's drive toward the East, forging close connections to important countries outside the orbit of America's domineering authority and control? Was the Saudi initiative a passing whim or a solid move to transform the entire basis of its pattern of its international relations? And how did the new trend of looking East influence Saudi Arabia's relationship with Asian, and especially East Asian, countries in practice?

The Saudi Looking-East: Sailing into uncharted waters?

Looking East means different things to different countries. While some nations have just recently mapped out a sort of looking-East orientation in their external affairs, there are other countries whose history of looking East harkens back to around half a century ago. And in sharp contrast to those countries for which looking East has been primarily about economic and financial gains, there are other nations for whom looking East means far more than politico-economic interests; their attention to the East has also had to do with identity, after making a fresh start in business and governance.[72] Interestingly, even within one country looking East can even mean different things at different points in time. For instance after its independence, India took a politico-ideologically pro-East policy by playing a leading role in the non-alignment movement. Since the early 1990s, however, India's looking-East approach is mainly aimed at economic and technological gains by building a relationship with a number of thriving nations in East Asia.

---

[71] Sean Foley, "Re-Orientalizing the Gulf: The GCC and Southeast Asia," *Middle East Policy*, Vol. 19, No. 4 (2012), pp. 77–87.

[72] James Fallows, *Looking at the Sun: The Rise of the New East Asian Economic and Political System* (New York: Vintage Books, 1995), p. 99–101.

This development took place even before the emerging India grew into a major international player.

The policy of looking-East in Saudi Arabia, however, seems to be something different. Back in the late 1990s, the then powerful Crown Prince Abdullah had been taken aback by China's swiftly emerging role and status in world politics.[73] Soon after ascending the throne in August 2005, King Abdullah paved the ground for closer ties with Asia in January 2006 by becoming the first Saudi ruler to visit China, one and half decades after the two nations had established official diplomatic ties in July 1990.[74]The Saudi–Indian relationship was also improved considerably under Abdullah, but Riyadh's growing connections to Beijing were what that made many in the West queasy about Saudi Arabia's new orientation toward the outside world.[75] The United States was suspicious about Abdullah's pro-Eastern proclivities, and this was probably one of the main reasons why Washington eventually took a firm stand against the Saudi king's desire to have his son Mutaib replace him; a bizarre scheme (given the ruling family's own conventional internal arrangements for power transition) which was to be later put into practice and rubber-stamped unequivocally by the Americans after the new king, Salman, astoundingly elevated his son, Mohammad, to the mighty position of crown prince in June 2017.

It's true that Abdullahh contributed significantly to Saudi Arabia's looking East, but his demise did not put an end to it. Despite their steadfast attachment to the West, the succeeding generation of Saudi leaders were not shy to demonstrate their willingness to develop better ties with Asian countries no matter how this was interpreted in Western policy circles. Moreover, the Saudi Arabian looking East was not intended to reverse its long-established reliance on the West. Nor did any influential Saudi dare to publicly brag about abandoning Washington or, generally, replacing the West with the East. In fact, since the formation of Saudi Arabia in September 1932 and the opening of the first American consulate in Dhahran in 1944, the Saudis had almost always regarded warm and congenial connections to Washington as the cornerstone of all Saudi security and foreign policies. This cardinal principle was accentuated all the more, now that the Saudi

---

[73] Robert Lacey, *Inside the Kingdom: Kings, Clerics, Modernists, Terrorists and the Struggle for Saudi Arabia* (London: Arrow Books, 2009), pp. 292–293.

[74] "Looking East: The Saudis are Hedging their Bets," *The Economist*, December 9, 2010.

[75] Stig Stenslie, *Regime Stability in Saudi Arabia: The Challenge of Succession* (Abingdon and New York: Routledge, 2012), pp. 12–13.

leaders were walking on eggshells trying to underscore the benign nature of their looking-East orientation.[76]

From the beginning, the Saudis wanted their looking-East approach serve two irreconcilable intentions. On one hand, the Saudi leaders desperately needed to show their Westerns allies that they had options, should circumstances require them to take a different course of action. For decades, successive American administrations had browbeaten the Saudis in various ways, making Saudi Arabia very insecure about the future of its political system and even its territorial integrity.[77] One American administration thought up plans to occupy the Saudi oil fields, while another administration threatened to raze to the ground the whole edifice of the Saudi monarchy.[78] One decade, the Saudi leaders feared that the West was probably planning to invade their country over human rights concerns, and another decade they worried about the ominous outcomes of their 9/11 dossier circulating in the corridors of power.[79] The Saudi leaders, therefore, needed a contingency plan, in case their country were put in serious jeopardy under any of those nightmarish scenarios.

On the other hand, Saudi Arabia did not really want its looking-East orientation to appear as a sort of "pivot to Asia." There were plenty of reasons for adopting a looking-East approach, but no one wanted to give the impression that this policy was going to replace the long-term attachment to the West. On the surface, "Looking East" was designed mainly to serve rather low-key political objectives, whereas its *raison d'être* was in fact to serve other undeclared and unadmitted objectives belonging to the realm of high politics. The Saudis knew full well that they were in no position to overtly engage in any kind of double game with the West, but latent perils were constantly lurking, and ties with the East could help serve as a kind of insurance policy. Saudi Arabia wished to retain its special place and the full confidence of American politicians across the political spectrum,[80] but it could no longer secure its vital interests in the familiar West without simultaneously venturing into the uncharted territory of the East.

---

[76] Robert Mason, *Foreign Policy in Iran and Saudi Arabia: Economics and Diplomacy in the Middle East* (London and New York: I.B. Tauris, 2015), pp. 77–78.

[77] Daryl Champion, "The Kingdom of Saudi Arabia: Elements of Instability within Stability," *Middle East Review of International Affairs*, Vol. 3, No. 4 (December 1999), pp. 49–73.

[78] Cooper, *The Oil Kings*, p. 116.

[79] James Wynbrandt, *A Brief History of Saudi Arabia* (New York: Facts On File, 2010), p. xii.

[80] Neil Partrick, ed., *Saudi Arabian Foreign Policy: Conflict and Cooperation* (London and New York: I.B. Tauris, 2016); and Craig Unger, *House of Bush, House of Saud: The Secret Relationship between the World's Two Most Powerful Dynasties* (New York: Scribner, 2004), pp. 79–81.

The politico-strategic ground: A shift in attitudes and perceptions

The American–Saudi Arabian alliance turned out to be one of the most critical bilateral relationships in contemporary international politics. This partnership between unlikely "friends" was essentially a marriage of convenience, meeting critical needs of both parties. It became particularly important when the Shah of Iran was toppled in the late 1970s, leaving one party at the whims of another. From the beginning, the United States had had its eye on the Saudi oil, as well as on the Saudi oil income.[81] As the archons of the capitalist system, the Americans required the constantly flowing Saudi crude to fuel the engines of their economic and industrial juggernauts.[82] Moreover, the United States developed a refined taste for Saudi Arabian petrodollars, using them to bankroll its own military-industrial complex through massive arms sales to the Saudis. These enormous sums of Saudi petrodollars also proved handy for financing America's endless overt and covert politico-military adventures in different parts of the world, particularly in the Middle East.[83]

For their part, the Saudis relied on the United States as the linchpin of their domestic stability and international reputation. A lot was at stake, and no country was in a better position than the United States to stand guard over Saudi Arabian territorial integrity in the long run. In fact, Saudi Arabia proved, on multiple occasions, to be an easy target for menacing domestic and regional threats, making its dependency on the United States a centerpiece of its foreign and security policies. In the pressure-cooker politics of Washington, however, nothing could be taken for granted, so that the Saudis were compelled to do their own heavy lifting by engaging in massive PR campaigns in every influential American institution, ranging from the two dominant political parties to private think tanks and from the media to academia.[84] This strategy was actually very effective for quite a long while, helping Saudi Arabia to win over Americans across the political spectrum, though the Saudis also benefited from the bloody and lengthy Iran–Iraq War

---

[81] Gerald Posner, *Secrets of the Kingdom: The Inside Story of the Secret Saudi–U.S. Connection* (New York: Random House, 2005).

[82] Roy, *Return of the Dragon*, pp. 174, 251.

[83] Pavel Stroilov, *Behind the Desert Storm: A Secret Archive Stolen from the Kremlin that Sheds New Light on the Arab Revolutions in the Middle East* (Chicago, IL: Price World Publishing, 2011), pp. 140, 155.

[84] Peter Schweizer, *Clinton Cash: The Untold Story of How and Why Foreign Governments and Businesses Helped Make Bill and Hillary Rich* (New York: HarperCollins Books, 2015); and Mitchell Bard, *The Arab Lobby: The Invisible Alliance that Undermines America's Interests in the Middle East* (New York: HarperCollins Publishers, 2010), pp. 67–71, 89.

as well as the successive West-led sanctions regimes imposed on Iraq and particularly Iran.[85]

The United States has become less dependent on Saudi Arabia in the past two decades, however, as the US was able to increase its own oil production, Iraqi oil flowed into the world markets in the wake of the dramatic invasion in 2003, and some American bases in the Middle East were strategically relocated.[86] On top of that, the American political establishment gradually became open and straightforward in demanding that the Saudi Arabian leadership implement certain reforms, in some cases reiterating urgent requests that had already been put forward by international institutions. Of course, in large measure the sharpening of American attitudes had to do with the rising tide of sulfurous opposition in the American media and public opinion regarding Saudi Arabia in the wake of the 9/11 incident.[87]

Meanwhile, serious disagreements over a whole host of regional issues brought American–Saudi Arabian frictions out into the open by the end of Barack Obama's two-term presidency. The Saudis had significant reservations about Washington's approach toward a number of Middle East countries, for instance Morsi's Egypt, in the aftermath of the so-called "Arab Spring" which in itself represented a possible threat to the Saudi Arabian political system.[88] A subsequent dispute over the ostensibly soft approach of the Obama administration to the Syrian civil war further damaged the Saudi–American partnership in the region.

But the one development that was perceived to be the most perilous to Saudi Arabia's interests was the surprising American willingness to engage in serious negotiations with Iran over its alleged nuclear program. That episode triggered alarm bells in Riyadh, causing near panic among the entire House of Saud. Any rapprochement between the Americans and Iranians could deal a major blow to Saudi Arabia's regional power and prestige, not to say to their very survival as a sovereign state.[89]

To guard their core interests and counterbalance any "sinister American move," therefore, the Saudis went surprisingly far out of their way in

---

[85] Steven Emerson, *The American House of Saud: The Secret Petrodollar Connection* (New York: Franklin Watts, 1985), p. 294.

[86] Brian Nugent, *In Defence of Conspiracy Theories: With Examples from Irish and International History and Politics* (London: Oldcastle, 2008), pp. 217, 228.

[87] Robert Baer, *Sleeping with the Devil: How Washington Sold Our Soul for Saudi Crude* (New York: Three Rivers Press, 2004); Vince Flynn, *Consent to Kill: A Thriller* (New York: Atria Books, 2008); and Marin Katusa, *The Colder War: How the Global Energy Trade Slipped from America's Grasp* (Hoboken, NJ: John Wiley & Sons, 2015), p. 208.

[88] Bruce D. Jones, *Still Ours to Lead: America, Rising Powers, and the Tension between Rivalry and Restraint* (Washington, D.C.: Brookings Institution Press, 2014), p. 51.

[89] Paul Aarts, "Saudi Arabia Walks the Tightrope," *The International Spectator*, Vol. 42, No. 4 (2007), pp. 545–550.

recalibrating some of the foundations of their foreign and security policies. They engaged in a number of clandestine meetings with their long-term arch enemy, Israel, and made some unprecedented conciliatory and cordial gestures toward the Russians. Saudi Arabia also lit a fresh fire under its looking-East program, particularly seeking to forge closer ties to China, because Riyadh's other important partners in the East were ultimately close allies of the United States. The Sino–Saudi relationship had already made significant progress after talks of forming a sort of strategic partnership between Beijing and Riyadh.[90] The new Saudi recourse to Beijing also dovetailed well with China's gigantic Belt and Road Initiative, which involved mega projects throughout the Middle East.

In fact, the regional factor had its own unique characteristics and significance. As noted, Saudi Arabia did not intend for its forays into the East (*xiang dong kan*) to compromise in any way the kingdom's fundamental looking-West (*xiang xi kan*) orientation. Nor did the Saudis expect to be included swiftly in the Chinese Communist Party's (CCP) "circle of friends" (*pengyou quan*).[91] The Saudis did not expect to be given anything on a silver platter; they simply wanted to make sure they did not lose any ground to their fierce regional rival, Iran, which had embarked in earnest upon a looking-East approach decades earlier. Now that Saudi Arabia was deeply anxious about the West's new penchant for playing up to Iran, other independent great powers like China might offer a much needed insurance policy.

Although the Chinese had driven a hard bargain with the Saudis in the early stage of the Syrian civil war,[92] China still shared with Saudi Araba some concerns about the unwelcome repercussions of a potential grand bargain between the West and Iran in the Middle East and beyond. This is one telling reason why the Saudis offered to the Chinese vast oil supplies and other sweetheart economic deals, hoping that China, as a member of the P5+1 group which was negotiating the nuclear deal with Iran, could nip it in the bud.[93]

---

[90] Evan S. Medeiros, *China's International Behavior: Activism, Opportunism, and Diversification* (Santa Monica, CA: Rand Corporation, 2009), p. 163.

[91] "Zhonggong 'pengyou quan' buduan kuoda" [The Chinese Communist Party's 'Circle of Friends' Keeps Expanding], *Renmin*, December 12, 2017.

[92] "Syrian Crisis will not Wreck Sino–Saudi Ties, Says Beijing," *Arab News*, May 15, 2012; "Gulf States Urge China to 'Reconsider Its Position'," *The National*, December 13, 2012; Christopher Phillips, *The Battle for Syria: International Rivalry in the New Middle East* (New Haven and London: Yale University Press, 2016), p. 92.

[93] Thomas W. Lippman, *Saudi Arabia on the Edge: The Uncertain Future of an American Ally* (Washington, D.C.: Potomac Books, 2012), p. 241; and Moritz Pieper, *Hegemony and Resistance around the Iranian Nuclear Programme: Analysing Chinese, Russian and Turkish Foreign Policies* (Abingdon and New York: Routledge, 2017).

Military engagement: A contingency plan to escape the defense dilemma

Saudi Arabia has long been a major purchaser of arms and sophisticated military equipment, allocating a fat budget for armaments one decade after another. In fact, their perennial penchant for procuring the latest technologies in foreign weapons and munitions has become almost legendary, outstripping the total defense spending of some great powers of the time.[94] In 2018, for instance, the military expenditure of Saudi Arabia ($82.9 billion) was the third largest in the world, ahead of Russia ($63.1 billion), Britain ($56.1 billion), and France ($53.4 billion), which were the world's fourth, sixth, and seventh biggest spenders, respectively.[95] Western countries, the United States in particular, have been the principal beneficiaries of the lucrative arms orders, enabling their own defense industries to survive and thrive during boom and bust. Of course, the hard-boiled Saudis are aware that they are being used as "cash cows," but they have had no other viable alternative to acquire sophisticated military equipment and at the same time ensure security coverage at other levels as well.[96]

Saudi Arabia uses these enormous deals as a bargaining chip with regard to a number of highly contentious policies and dubious deeds the Arab country is often held accountable for. For many decades, the weight of weapons acquisitions helped the Saudis to effectively skirt a great deal of scathing criticism. But when the deluge of pressure seemed to approach the point of no return, the Saudis needed to think up additional contingency plans. Although Saudi Arabia was unable to completely block any severe recrimination against its policy behaviors, Riyadh could still intimidate its powerful arms suppliers in the West by threatening significant cutbacks in these purchases.[97]

Diversification in sourcing military equipment could therefore provide the Saudis with a bit of flexibility, even if the West was, for now, the best market for advanced armaments. The West's commitment to their overall security and military considerations had begun to look shaky.[98] Moreover, a

---

[94] Emerson, p. 54; and Stephan Stetter, *The Middle East and Globalization: Encounters and Horizons* (New York: Palgrave Macmillan, 2012), p. 34.

[95] International Institute for Strategic Studies (IISS), *The Military Balance 2019* (London: Routledge, 2019).

[96] Bruce Riedel, *Kings and Presidents: Saudi Arabia and the United States since FDR* (Washington, D.C.: Brookings Institution Press, 2017), p. 200.

[97] David B. Ottaway, *The King's Messenger: Prince Bandar Bin Sultan, and America's Tangled Relationship with Saudi Arabia* (New York: Walker & Company: 2008); and Bard, p. 69.

[98] "China May Seek to Boost Ties with Saudi Arabia but It 'Can't Fill US Arms Sales Gap'," *South China Morning Post*, October 17, 2018.

growing number of alternative weaponry producers were appearing, whet-
ting the Saudis' appetite for cheaper equipment, which Eastern countries
were more than happy to provide — without any strings attached. Not only
did the Saudis have more say in deciding the type and size of the weapons
they could purchase in the East, they could use such deals to promote bilateral connections to Eastern countries in other critical economic and technological areas.

Saudi Arabia's arms engagement with Asian countries actually preceded
its looking-East orientation. The practice was in place a few years before
the Arab kingdom normalized its diplomatic relations with China in 1990.[99]
It was around 1986 when a Saudi official purchased, albeit in a clandestine
manner, some 25 intercontinental ballistic missiles (CSS2s) from China in
the wake of the Iran–Iraq War which had opened the door for the interna-
tionalization of the Chinese arms industry. China had managed to supply a
significant load of armaments to both warring parties during that internecine conflict, arousing the curiosity of the Saudi leadership. They wanted
to get their hands on some of this Chinese weaponry regardless of the fact
that diplomatic relations were blocked due to Riyadh's official ties to Taipei.
Interestingly, more than two decades later, in 2007, the Saudis purchased
some Dongfeng 21 missiles from China, again clandestinely,[100] in part because
Beijing's ongoing military cooperation with Saudi Arabia's arch-rival Iran
had left them eager to stay up to date with the nuts and bolts of Chinese
military hardware entering the Middle East.

The Chinese, therefore, became the main partner for military and defense
cooperation in Saudi Arabia's looking-East approach. Over time, the Saudis
also managed to develop military and defense relationships with some other
important players in Asia, including India, Japan, and South Korea.[101] But the
Saudis always felt an agonizing concern that all of these were close allies

---

[99] The communist China under Mao had actually invited Saudi Arabia's Prince Faisal to
visit Beijing in mid-1950s, but King Saud had turned down the Chinese invitation. See:
Parker T. Hart, *Saudi Arabia and the United States: Birth of a Security Partnership* (Bloomington,
IN: Indiana University Press, 1998), p. 65.

[100] The Sino–Saudi disguised deal in 2007 was reportedly brokered with Washington's
tacit approval because the American CIA needed to make sure that Saudi Arabia was not
going to eventually engage in a Pakistan-style quest to nuclearize by taking advantage of
the relevant nuclear technologies supplied by China. For more details, see: "Exclusive:
CIA Helped Saudis in Secret Chinese Missile Deal," *Newsweek*, January 29, 2014; and
Nicholas L. Miller and Tristan A. Volpe, "Abstinence or Tolerance: Managing Nuclear
Ambitions in Saudi Arabia," *The Washington Quarterly*, Vol. 41, No. 2 (2018), pp. 27–46.

[101] "Boost to Defense Ties with India," *Arab News*, February 14, 2012; "Riyadh, Seoul Boost
Defense Cooperation," *Arab News*, February 5, 2013; "India, Saudi Arabia Sign Defense
Agreement," *Al-Arabiya*, February 28, 2014; "Japan Maritime Squadrons to Participate
in Joint Exercise," *Arab News*, November 12, 2014; and "Riyadh, Seoul to Bolster Defense
Ties," *Arab News*, January 1, 2015.

of the United States and therefore could be subject to Washington's arm-twisting at any moment, should Washington change its attitude toward Saudi Arabia.[102] Under such a ghastly disturbing scenario, none of those three Asian nations would be able to stand by any defense and military agreements with the Saudis. By comparison, China was in a position to serve as a resourceful purveyor of armaments in the short term and the long term as well.

Petroleum plus: In search of riches and recognition

As the largest exporter of crude oil in the world, Saudi Arabia presently pumps more than 10 million barrels of petroleum per day.[103] They possess around 18 percent of the world's proven oil reserves, and this is granting them a special place in all international energy calculations. Oil played an indispensable role in the survival of the Saudi monarchy and its distinctive style of domestic control and policymaking for more than half a century.[104] It is oil that gives Saudi Arabia a strong say in regional and international developments.[105] As a "swing producer," Saudi Arabia has turned out to be an especially salient element in determining the stability of oil prices and thereby affecting the international economy. In this way, the Saudis have contributed to the success of many international policies carved out by the US-led West, including in the Middle East.[106]

Meanwhile, during the past two decades Saudi Arabia gradually encountered a number of menacing challenges, calling into question its enviable position in the international oil markets. The kingdom's regional status and role were affected as well. A new oil boom in the United States, the rise of new petroleum producers in different parts of the world, a boost in the output of other sources of energy other than crude oil and natural gas, and volatility in international oil prices all put the Saudis in a difficult situation.[107] In the twilight zone of energy speculations, however, Asia remained the up-and-coming region for the future of Saudi oil exports. Over time, Saudi Arabia

---

[102] "Qingdao' Warship Berths in Jeddah Port for Rest," *People's Daily*, May 3, 2012; and "Saudi Arabia Pivots to Asia (For Now)," *The Diplomat*, March 30, 2017.

[103] It may sound counterintuitive, but Saudi Arabia is also one of the largest oil consumers in the world, ahead of industrialized giants such as Germany and South Korea. See: Rory Miller, *Desert Kingdoms to Global Powers: The Rise of the Arab Gulf* (New Haven, CT: Yale University Press, 2016), p. 223.

[104] Ross, *The Oil Curse*, p. 124.

[105] Alastair Crooke, "You Can't Understand ISIS If You Don't Know the History of Wahhabism in Saudi Arabia," *New Perspectives Quarterly*, Vol. 32, No. 1 (2015), pp. 56–70.

[106] Cooper, p. 206.

[107] "Low Oil Prices Spur the Saudis to Play the Field," *The New York Times*, February 26, 2018, p. A1.

shipped less and less crude oil to Western countries, while it managed to comfortably replace the loss by supplying more oil to the quickly developing Asian nations. This was another reason why the Saudis needed to double down on their looking-East orientation.[108]

In fact, Riyadh's growing connections to the East helped position Saudi Arabia as China's principal purveyor of petroleum by the early twenty-first century. A seismic shift took place when they managed to ship more than half of their crude oil exports to Asia alone, before the first decade of the century was actually over. The Saudis were now obviously selling more petroleum to China than to the United States.[109] The prospect of shipping larger cargoes of crude oil to India was equally bright; nevertheless, the Saudis preferred to foster closer ties with the Chinese, whose economy is larger. They are hugely dependent on imported energy, and their hands-off approach to foreign policy further buoys up the Saudi determination for forging strategic oil cooperation with Beijing. Consequently, Saudi Arabia's giant oil corporation, Aramco, was tasked with purchasing more stakes in Chinese refineries, while China was encouraged to simultaneously pour more capital and technology into joint refinery projects across the Arab kingdom.[110]

Saudi Arabia had certainly been a long-term supplier of crude oil to the East, and the rise of new powerhouses like China and India increased its interest in the region. Still, the US-led international sanctions against Iran dovetailed neatly with the Saudis' desire to safeguard their rising stakes in the East. The more the West tightened its screws on Iran, the more Saudi Arabia became critical to the energy security of the oil-hungry countries of Asia. In particular, when the punitive sanctions targeted the Iranian oil industry, Saudi Arabia was in a better position to make up the energy loss caused by the interruption in Iran's crude exports. The Saudis knew that the positive impact of the episode could be partly temporary, but they were determined to make most of it by attempting to wean the thirsty Asian oil customers away from Iran, and at any rate, to earn more petrodollars by shipping more crude oil to Asia. They also sought to secure new long-term contracts in other non-energy sectors.

Second, the Saudis wanted to turn their petroleum role into a larger strategic asset in the East and, generally, in international politics. Perceiving itself as the "shock absorber" of the world's energy markets, Saudi Arabia wished

---

[108] Matthew R. Simmons, *Twilight in the Desert: The Coming Saudi Oil Shock and the World Economy* (Hoboken, NJ: John Wiley & Sons, 2005), p. 115; and Robert Vitalis, *America's Kingdom: Mythmaking on the Saudi Oil Frontier* (Stanford, CA: Stanford University Press, 2007), pp. 102, 259.

[109] Katusa, p. 207; and Jones, *Still Ours to Lead*, p. 52.

[110] Shapiro, *Futurecast*, p. 274.

to be acknowledged and appreciated *pari passu* with its "unique contribution" to the stability and prosperity of the international economy.[111] The Saudis expected their close partners in the East to press the West, either implicitly or explicitly, not to have any malign design against the Arab country. Since the oil-dependent Asian countries were already very dependent on the Saudis for their energy security, their strong endorsement and open backing could effectively buttress the position of the Saudis in the West.

The building bonanza: Construction as bait on the hook

Oil has indubitably been a prominent element behind Saudi Arabia's expanding relations with the East; nevertheless, the kingdom's construction industry has also played an instrumental role linking the two sides over several decades. Because of the power of crude exports as the *fons et origo* to fill the Saudi state's coffers, Saudi Arabia, like some other petroleum producers in the Middle East, has always had the option of splashing reserves of petrodollars on construction projects. Moreover, the Saudi looking-East orientation, in its tranquil pace, roughly coincided with another windfall in oil income when petroleum prices hit a record high of $147 a barrel on June 11, 2008. The Saudis decided to use the occasion as a boost for their new approach toward the Asian countries. The previous oil boom (1974–1985) had actually turned Saudi Arabia into the largest construction market and the *ne plus ultra* of overseas building for close to one and half decades, drawing into the Arab kingdom a whole host of Asian companies, both public and private, in addition to hundreds of thousands of Asian manual laborers.[112]

It was in the aftermath of the first oil shock in 1973 when a slew of Japanese, Taiwanese and, especially, Korean contractors moved to Saudi Arabia to build the Arab kingdom's massive projects. That halcyon period lasted almost until 1986, and it still never dwindled to a trickle. This in turn made a huge contribution to South Korea's industrialization and economic development in various ways.[113] As a case in point, Saudi Arabia's Jubail project in 1979 made the Korean Hyundai the largest construction company in the world, as the value of the sweetheart deal was equivalent to half of South Korea's gross national product (GNP) at the time.[114] On top of that, the construction boom

---

[111] "Saudi Arabia is World's Energy 'Shock Absorber', Says Minister Al-Falih," *Arab News*, October 15, 2018.

[112] Friedemann Bartu, *The Ugly Japanese: Nippon's Economic Empire in Asia* (Singapore: Longman, 1992), p. 59.

[113] Shirzad Azad, *Koreans in the Persian Gulf: Policies and International Relations* (Abingdon and New York: Routledge, 2015), p. 41.

[114] Richard M. Steers, *Made in Korea: Chung Ju Yung and the Rise of Hyundai* (New York: Routledge, 1999), pp. 116–117.

paved the way for a long-term engagement of the East Asian countries in Saudi Arabia because of their enthusiasm to invest considerably in the Saudi energy and other EPC (engineering, procurement, and construction) projects. China was significantly missing in that first, highly profitable period; however, it later made the most of the following boom season (almost from 2010 onward) in the Saudi construction industry.[115]

In sharp contrast to other Asian companies, the determined and dedicated Chinese set foot in Saudi Arabia's bustling construction market with one master plan after another. A decade after embarking upon its vaunted "going out" (*zou chuqu*) strategy, China under the leadership of Xi Jinping came up with the "One Belt, One Road" (OBOR or *yidai yilu*) initiative, drawing a bead on Saudi Arabia as a major partner for its mega projects in the Middle East.[116] The Chinese soon proposed and then launched the Asian Infrastructure Investment Bank (AIIB), convincing the Saudis to join the flourishing framework as an important stakeholder. Capitalizing on Saudi Arabia's looking-East drive and the "2030 Vision," Chinese officials often strived to convince the Saudis that their plans were all on the same wavelength.[117] In addition to encouraging their companies to address the Saudi projects in a dedicated and efficient way, the Chinese also called on Saudi Arabia to overcome the sporadic troubles triggered by its guest workers by making more use of China's abundant pool of unskilled workers.

Technology transfer: Industrial diversification as a royal remedy

Over the course of several decades, Asian countries persistently poured capital as well as expertise and technical know-how into Saudi Arabia's energy and construction industries. Apart from the whopping profits, their objective was primarily to cushion against a potential interruption of crude supply from the Arab kingdom.[118] This strategy was particularly exploited by those Asian countries which were more susceptible to dicey politico-economic conditions and precarious energy flows. A case in point is the Republic of China (Taiwan), which benefited hugely from this stratagem both prior to and after the breaking off of official diplomatic relations with

---

[115] "Construction in the Middle East is Booming again," *Business Insider*, October 8, 2013.

[116] Arthur R. Kroeber, *China's Economy: What Everyone Needs to Know* (New York: Oxford University Press, 2016), p. 242; and "For China, the Belt and Road Run through the Middle East, *South China Morning Post*, July 14, 2018.

[117] "China Sees Saudi Arabia as Important Partner in Belt and Road Construction: Chinese FM," *Xinhua*, May 22, 2018; and "The Belt and Road Initiative + Saudi Vision 2030 — Endowing China–Saudi Arabia Cooperation with New Opportunities and Broad Prospects," *Ministry of Foreign Affairs, the People's Republic of China*, October 1, 2018.

[118] Simmons, p. 348.

Saudi Arabia in the early 1990s. In order to curry favor with the Saudis in all crucial energy and commercial areas, the Taiwanese government was willing to provide technological products and engineering services which the Saudis could not get easily or cheaply from other sources.[119] In fact, the tiny East Asian state's varied technological connections to the Middle East country covered fields ranging from agricultural and fishing applications to medical and marketing training.[120]

As part of its new looking-East approach, however, Saudi Arabia has strived to turn to good use its connections to Asian nations in other fields as well. A number of alarming domestic challenges have compelled it to think up a major policy of industrial diversification to reduce its over-dependence on oil incomes.[121] The "2030 Vision" emerged as the warp and woof of this master plan, with the optimistic aim of accelerating Saudi Arabia's drive toward a knowledge-based economy of sorts. Instead of being content with their international status as a producer of petroleum, the Saudis sought to one day become a major hub for exporting renewables in the world.[122] But Saudi Arabia's traditional allies in the West were probably reluctant to give them all-out assistance with these ambitious objectives.[123] The Arab kingdom was ultimately dependent on its Asian partners to make a name for itself by utilizing their knowledge, skills, and technology.[124]

Before being courted by Saudi Arabia for its new technology-oriented economic transformation, however, many Asian countries were already competing with each other in the Middle East in providing the industrial experience and technical know-how the region desperately required.[125] The field of nuclear energy was particularly hot and itself triggered a fresh rivalry among resourceful Asian countries active throughout the region. For example, South Korea had agreed to build a number of nuclear reactors

---

[119] Cooper, p. 160.

[120] "Taiwanese Products Impress Saudi Traders," *Saudi Gazette*, June 14, 2014.

[121] Leif Wenar, *Blood Oil: Tyrants, Violence, and the Rules that Run the World* (New York: Oxford University Press, 2016), p. 94.

[122] Felix Wilde, *Worldwide Development of Nuclear Energy: Strategic Deployment of German Consultancies in the Arabian Market* (Hamburg: Diplomica Verlag GmbH, 2011), p. 24; and Christopher M. Schroeder, *Startup Rising: The Entrepreneurial Revolution Remaking the Middle East* (New York: Palgrave Macmillan, 2013), p. 104.

[123] "Blocking Saudi nuclear plant opens door to China, Perry says," *Bloomberg*, March 22, 2018; and "GOP senators press Trump to halt nuclear energy talks with Saudi Arabia," *The Hill*, October 31, 2018.

[124] "Tokyo Offers Riyadh Nuclear Power Help," *Arab News*, February 11, 2013; "Kingdom, China Reach Technology Transfer Accord for 'Made in Makkah' Project," *Arab News*, November 17, 2013; and "Saudi, Korean Firms to Build Car Manufacturing Plant," *Arab News*, May 16, 2015.

[125] The World Bank, *Strengthening China's and India's Trade and Investment Ties to the Middle East and North Africa* (Washington, D.C.: The World Bank, 2009), pp. 85–88.

for the United Arab Emirates, while Japan and Turkey were in the midst of intense negotiations over an identical area of strategic economic coopera-tion.[126] In the same way, Saudi Arabia was planning to construct 16 nuclear reactors by 2030, wishing to have South Korea, Japan, and particularly China as major stakeholders in its drive toward achieving nuclear energy.[127] If Asian countries could lend a helping hand to Saudi Arabia in this critical and hazardous field, they would be, in all likelihood, prepared to accommodate the Saudis with some other less contentious areas of technological collabora-tion as well.

Imports: Switching partners and products

In the face of all the talk and pledges about the urgency and significance of economic diversification, crude oil has remained the mainstay of the Saudi Arabian economy and the major source of financing for its immense imports. In the period after the first oil shock of 1973, when petroleum was undeni-ably the lynch pin of the kingdom's international commerce, the Saudis often contemplated finding ways to lessen their over-dependence on oil incomes.[128] Of course, almost all oil producers in the world have sought to diversify, especially when petroleum prices became highly volatile.[129] Still, unlike many other oil producers, the Saudis had little else, if anything, to export, and erratic oil prices could deal a severe blow to their national budget and exorbitantly foreign expenditures. The bill for the humongous imports was particularly a bugbear of the Saudi government because the more barrels of crude oil Saudi Arabia exported, the larger the load of commodity cargoes it imported correspondingly.[130]

Moreover, Saudi Arabia used to purchase the bulk of its imports from Western countries, the United States in particular. The Saudis had to rely on imported Western products of every type, from advanced weaponry to basic food stuff. This situation, however, began to change substantially as Saudi Arabia engaged in higher volumes of commerce with Eastern coun-tries, particularly China. Sino–Saudi bilateral trade jumped from a meager

---

[126] "Japan, Turkey Ink $22 Billion Nuclear Plant Deal," *The Japan Times*, May 4, 2013.

[127] "Saudi Plans to Build 16 Nuclear Reactors by 2030," *Reuters*, June 1, 2011; "KSA Explores Atomic Energy Cooperation with Japan," *Arab News*, July 5, 2015; and "'Made in China' Nuclear Reactors a Tough Sell in Global Market," *Reuters*, March 6, 2015.

[128] Jared Rubin, *Rulers, Religion, and Riches: Why the West Got Rich and the Middle East Did Not* (New York: Cambridge University Press, 2017), p. 214.

[129] "Lower Oil Prices Force Saudis to Widen Their Circle of Friends," *The New York Times*, February 25, 2018.

[130] Robert E. Looney, "Saudi Arabian Budgetary Dilemmas," *Middle Eastern Studies*, Vol. 26, No. 1 (1990), pp. 76–87.

$290 million in 1990 to $60 billion by the end of 2011. At this point, China overtook the United States as the Arab kingdom's largest trading partner.[131] Saudi Arabia was supplying larger cargoes of crude oil to China and other Asian countries, but that was not all. The changing dynamic of the Saudi international commerce also stemmed from the fact that China and some other Asian nations were now shipping to Saudi Arabia massive quantities of low-cost goods, including electronics, textiles, toys, and food stuffs. For decades, the citizens of Saudi Arabia had been used to buying cutting edge commodities from the West, and it was not easy for all of them to adjust their tastes to the similar but subpar products from the East, no matter if many well-to-do Muslim pilgrims of the "Hajj economy" were more than happy to bargain over a sundry of exotic souvenirs made by Asian countries.[132]

A growing proportion of Saudi Arabia's population, however, had little option but to depend on the imported Asian products. Like poor migrant workers from other countries, Saudi Arabia's own lower and even middle-income families increasingly became the main customers of those low-priced goods imported from Asia.[133] Additionally, ongoing economic reforms and social transformations are anticipated to gradually and inevitably increase the class divide, leading to an increase in the percentage of lower-income and poor people.[134]

The looking-East orientation fortuitously made progress in tandem with this crucial domestic development. As Saudi Arabia has developed closer connections to more countries in the East and supplied them with larger cargoes of crude oil, it needs to bring back part of the growing revenues through importing goods produced by those Asian oil customers. And then there is the fiduciary responsibility of the Saudi government to try everything at its disposal, including cultural means, in order to persuade people from all social strata in the Arab kingdom to buy the vast quantities of new imported Asian products.

Culture: From Hajj diplomacy to Hallyu frenzy

Culture has long played an instrumental role in smoothing the way for better politico-economic tie-ins between Saudi Arabia and its Asian counterparts. In contemporary history, however, it was Asian countries which first capitalized on culture in order to grease the wheels of their expanding

[131] Mason, p. 79.
[132] "Made in China' Label Discourages Saudis," *Arab News*, January 22, 2014.
[133] The World Bank, *Strengthening China's and India's Trade and Investment*, p. 21.
[134] Stetter, p. 69; and Jonathan J. Pierce, "Oil and the House of Saud: Analysis of Saudi Arabian Oil Policy," *Digest of Middle East Studies*, Vol. 21, No. 1 (2012), pp. 89–107.

commercial machine in countries such as Saudi Arabia. They launched a number of academic and cultural bodies to foster among their interested population a basic understanding about the Arabic language and Islamic cultural mores.[135] More importantly, almost all Asian countries with significantly rising stakes in Saudi Arabia took advantage of their Muslim minorities to promote more friendly interactions with the Saudis.[136] Influential and cooperative people among the minority Muslim groups were particularly beneficial in facilitating informal diplomacy between Asian authorities and their counterparts in Saudi Arabia.[137] The frequent pilgrimages of those pious people to the Arab country's holy shrines could also be used as a sort of "Hajj diplomacy" by using the occasion for signing political agreements as well as business contracts.[138]

Although different cultural measures initiated by Asian countries helped them greatly to improve their own knowledge and perceptions about Saudi Arabia, and the Middle East in general, those initiatives did little to help the Saudis to learn about Asian politico-economic and cultural systems. By the time Riyadh ventured onto its new course of looking East, the Saudis still lacked much practical understanding about their key partners in the East. Saudi Arabia had invested heavily in securing and promoting its deep interest in the West, through cultural means in addition to other methods. But the Saudis had fallen behind in boosting their own image in the East or updating their own feeble grasp of Asian countries.[139] The average citizens of Saudi Arabia, like their political elites, were in need of a basic working understanding of the rising East.

As part of its looking-East approach, therefore, Saudi Arabia resorted to some new cultural strategies. Education and media were considered to be

---

[135] Sending students and scholars to study and research in major Middle Eastern countries was also part of this important approach.

[136] Of course, for some Asian countries such as China the Muslim minority could sometimes easily become a double-edged sword and a source of menacing trouble of any kind. See: "Al Qaeda Vows Revenge on China over Uyghur Deaths," *Daily Telegraph*, July 14, 2009; and "Al-Qaeda Magazine Calls for Xinjiang to be 'Recovered by the Islamic Caliphate'," *South China Morning Post*, October 21, 2014.

[137] "Minjian waijiao' lajin 'zhongguo musilinsheng' yu musilinguojiao de juli" ['People's Diplomacy' Has Lessened Distance between 'China's Muslim Province' and Muslim Nations], *Renmin*, May 10, 2008.

[138] "Revenue from Pilgrims Make 3% of Saudi GDP," *Arab News*, January 5, 2013.

[139] Of course, the Saudi government had occasionally offered ready cash or donated some lofty gifts to the construction and maintenance of mosques and Islamic bodies in different Asian countries. Contribution to the Asian victims of some natural disasters or man-made tragedies used to also be another cultural activity of Saudi Arabia, but such generous actions hardly created a lasting positive image of the Arab kingdom among average Asian citizens, nor those deeds, regardless of their short-term impacts, could improve markedly the Saudi leaders' own overall knowledge and understanding about Asian countries.

particularly effective tools to quickly (if partially) fill the gap. Many students were sponsored by the Saudi government, through generous scholarships and financial aids, to study in Asian countries. In doing do, the priority was given to those East Asian countries which had more advanced and sophisticated educational institutions, in order to train a greater number of competent graduates for the Arab kingdom. As a result, more and more undergraduate and graduate students from Saudi Arabia have been encouraged to apply for various Japanese, South Korean, Chinese, and even Indian universities and colleges over the past two decades.[140] This Saudi move is also aimed to compete with a similar trend among some other Middle Eastern countries which have by far a larger community of students studying and working throughout Asia.

Regarding the media and entertainment industry, Saudi Arabia unexpectedly paved the way for the promotion of Asian cultural products in the kingdom. A growing number of Asian movies and dramas were dubbed into the Arabic language and then broadcast through the public TV channels throughout the Arab country. The Korean wave particularly found the Saudi soil to be fertile ground for *Hallyu's* entertaining products, which soon turned out to be a big hit.[141] Many intrigued youth and teenagers in Saudi Arabia subsequently subscribed to learning the Korean language and practicing Taekwondo, while more households gradually became interested in purchasing different Korean brands.[142] This came to be seen as a good lesson for other aspiring Asian countries, like China and India, which acknowledged that culture could be a powerful medium to further their expanding presence in the Arab kingdom.[143]

Conclusion

The looking-East orientation has indeed animated Saudi Arabian foreign policy making and international relations. For more than half a century, the close alliance with Western countries, the United States in particular,

---

[140] "More Saudi Students Opting for S. Korea," *Arab News*, June 26, 2014; "600 Saudi Students Currently Studying in Japanese Universities," *Arab News*, December 15, 2014; and "Number of Students Studying in India Grows," *Arab News*, April 5, 2015.

[141] Aside from cultural and economic realms, Saudi Arabia's looking-East orientation contributed considerably to the political, and even military and technological, aspects of bilateral relations between Riyadh and Seoul. As a case in point, in 2007 and after a hiatus of some 27 years, Roh Moo-hyun became the first South Korean president to visit Saudi Arabia since the last state visit conducted by Choi Kyu-hah in 1980.

[142] "Korean Wave Makes a Splash Worldwide," *Financial Times*, August 23, 2017; and "Saudi Girls Catch 'K' Fever," *Arab News*, January 8, 2018.

[143] Joel Wuthnow, "The Concept of Soft Power in China's Strategic Discourse," *Issues and Studies*, Vol. 44, No. 2 (2008), pp. 1–28.

served as the cornerstone of Saudi Arabia's approach to the outside world. Almost in every important aspect of foreign and security matters, the Saudis used to consult with their Western allies before making decisions. This modus operandi also colored Saudi Arabia's image among other countries in the Middle East and beyond. In contrast to its West-oriented pattern of security and foreign policy making, Saudi Arabia's looking-East drive was essentially meant to broaden the scope of its interactions with the outside world. A confluence of external and internal parameters had cautioned the Saudis about the potential perils of over-dependence on the West, compelling them to look for ways to foster closer connections to the East.

The Saudi Arabian looking-East policy inevitably brought about new dynamics in the Arab kingdom's relationship with many Asian countries. In fact, it turned Saudi Arabia's half-hearted links to Asian nations into effective multifaceted connections, encompassing all politico-strategic, military, economic, technological, and cultural spheres. In addition to making up for shortcomings and limitations in Saudi Arabia's earlier ties with Asian countries, the looking-East approach sets its sights on cultivating mutual symbiotic interactions between the Saudis and their Asian partners over the long haul. Saudi Arabia's initiatives, moreover, received strong support by the East as some of Asian countries, like China, were already waiting in the wings to advance their growing interests in the kingdom.

Additionally, Saudi Arabia's looking-East move had considerable impact on its Arab, and especially the Gulf Cooperation Council (GCC), partners in the Middle East and North African region. As the GCC's *primus inter pares*, Saudi Arabia has long played a pivotal role in setting important agendas, formulating ecumenical policies, and implementing compelling strategies within the Arab bloc, regardless of the recent open hostilities between Doha and Riyadh. These small and susceptible states all shared in common a great deal of Saudi Arabia's security and foreign policy priorities. For this reason, the junior partners of the GCC were justifiably poised to take a leaf out of Saudi Arabia's looking-East book. The commonality of interests fitted neatly into the Middle East policies of many Asian countries which were just in search of new strategies to expand their politico-economic footprint throughout the region. It was thereby highly convenient for them to come up with a set of similar policies and strategies toward the GCC countries in order to turn the Saudi-led looking-East initiative to their own advantage.

CHAPTER 3. UNITED ARAB EMIRATES: RIDING ON THE CREST OF EASTERN WAVES

Taking inspiration from Saudi Arabia's successful strategic-diplomatic overtures, the smaller members of the Gulf Cooperation Council (GCC), too, have been seeking broader partnerships with the East over the past two decades. Saudi Arabia had long served as a role model for these smaller countries. Some of the smaller partners of the GCC had certainly a long history of politico-economic interactions with Asia, but new circumstances required them to diversify and broaden their existing connections to more Asian countries.

While some other smaller members of the GCC, like Kuwait, enjoyed a longer political history of independence and more enduring trade relationship with the East, the UAE is the second largest economy in the GCC after Saudi Arabia and its economy is far more diversified than all the other members of that regional bloc.

Moreover, the location of the UAE's important port cities has enabled the country to serve as a gateway to many other GCC states. Despite the UAE's short history and small size, this advantage has given it an instrumental role linking much of the commercial and financial interactions between the GCC countries and their partners across the world.[144]

Given these favorable circumstances, most, if not all, major trading nations of the East were willing to court the tiny Arab country. With Asian countries wanting good relations for the sake of easier and more efficient

---

[144] Kenneth Christie, "Globalisation, Religion and State Formation in the United Arab Emirates and Pakistan," *Totalitarian Movements and Political Religions*, Vol. 11, No. 2 (2010), pp. 203–212.

commercial connections, would the UAE require a separate Looking-East agenda of its own? What was the essence of "Looking East" from an Emirati perspective, and how did the Emirati looking East actually play out?

The Emirati looking-East: Securing a position of advantage

Since its formal establishment in 1971, a coordinated coalition of seven emirates has dominated the political dynamics in the UAE, determining the Arab federation's socio-political and cultural interactions. Originating in tribalism and tribal proclivities, the legitimacy of the ruling elites in regulating and managing the state affairs has not been seriously challenged over the course of half a century, largely because an overwhelming majority of the country's residents are foreigners. Only a tiny minority of its population are regarded as bona fide citizens.[145]

During the past several decades, moreover, the indigenous population has benefited greatly from the country's astonishing new-found wealth, which in turn has further legitimized the policies and procedures its parvenu rulers have carved out and implemented steadfastly. The average Emirati citizen has been catapulted, in the space of one or two generations, from the life of a desperate desert dweller into a modern professional and an occupant of a spectacular skyscraper well equipped with all the trappings of luxury and comfort.

Externally, the UAE's foreign policy has been built on the basis of close and cordial relations with the fellow Arabs in the GCC and some other parts of the Middle East and North African (MENA) region. Still, what has formed the backbone of the UAE's foreign and security policies is a special alliance with a number of Western countries, the United States in particular.[146] In fact, this attachment has played a crucial role in the calculus of the UAE's overall interactions with the outside world, directing the Arab state's politico-economic connections to many other countries in addition to contributing tremendously to its domestic affluence and international standing.[147] For a whole host of regional and international reasons, however, in the post-Cold War era the U.S. factor in the UAE's pivotal foreign and security considerations has grown steadily and extensively, while the erst-

---

[145] Miller, *Desert Kingdoms to Global Powers*, p. 6.
[146] Lake, *Hierarchy in International Relations*, p. 89.
[147] Marc J. O'Reilly, *Unexceptional: America's Empire in the Persian Gulf, 1941–2007* (Lanham, MD: Lexington Books, 2008), p. 291.

while significance of some major European partners for the Arab country has been declining in favor of new stakeholders from the East.[148]

Above all, shrinking economic and financial opportunities have reduced Europe to a secondary importance to the Emirati leadership; and that is precisely what made the rising Asian powers alluring and appealing. The East seemed to abound with huge opportunities, especially economically and financially, convincing the UAE to prepare to refocus eastward in the long term. The developed and industrialized parts of East Asia had already benefited the UAE considerably, and a swiftly industrializing and growing China promised even more opportunities.[149] The Indian elephant was to soon join the Chinese dragon, suggesting that a long era of Asian boom and plenty was in the offing. One crucial factor driving a commitment to looking East in the UAE was, therefore, the growing politico-economic and technological capabilities of the rising Asian powers. These emerging economic power-houses were destined to be a new fountainhead of investment and economic gains, signifying the plausibility and potential fruitfulness of a looking-East orientation.[150]

Another equally critical rationale for looking East had to do with the UAE's perception of its favorable status in the region and the way a prom-ising East could strengthen it in long haul. The surprise rise of the UAE itself had taken place under fortuitous circumstances, and it appeared to the Emiratis that there was going to be no better blueprint to secure their new position and prosperity than to take advantage of a quickly rising Asia and channel some of its benefits and rewards. The UAE was actually striving to secure its unique niche, and probably only the up-and-coming Asian giants had the wherewithal to make its dreams come true. Moreover, the successful implementation of a looking-East approach could even boost the legitimacy and popularity of the Emirati ruling class. In that sense, they had something in common with some of their Eastern counterparts whose reputation and approval greatly hinge on maintaining a continuous pace of development and progress.

The politico-strategic landscape: Toward complex partnership

Over the past two decades, an intricate network of relations has evolved between the UAE and its American and Asian partners. The tiny Arab state

---

[148] Christopher M. Davidson, "Dubai and the United Arab Emirates: Security Threats," *British Journal of Middle Eastern Studies*, Vol. 36, No. 3 (2009), pp. 431–447.

[149] "Message from Consul-General of United Arab Emirates," *South China Morning Post*, April 21, 2015.

[150] Miller, p. 280; and Parker, "China's Growing Interests in the Persian Gulf."

gradually emerged as a cornerstone of the U.S. policy in the Persian Gulf region after the Iraq War of 2003. Close interactions and frequent consultations between the Americans and their Emirati partners had certainly far-reaching implications extending to other parts of the Middle East and beyond.[151] The United States surprisingly regarded the UAE as an important partner, as the alliance between Washington and Abu Dhabi expanded to address a whole array of regional and even international issues.[152] For obvious reasons, part of the growing significance of the UAE to the United States stemmed from the expanding role and influence of Asian powers in the region amid Abu Dhabi's own parallel diplomacy to foster closer relations with the East. One peculiar aspect of the situation was the UAE's drive to engage in diverse connections to Washington's allies in Asia and its adversaries as well, which seemed to go forward since the Emiratis already had the blessing of the Americans with regard to their murky maneuvers toward the East.

The UAE's politico-diplomatic relationship with India grew by leaps and bounds. Since the early 2000s, the two sides exchanged several high-level talks and official visits, leading to a strategic engagement between Abu Dhabi and New Delhi. Important benefits accrued to both parties due to their good relationship in many areas. In addition, the UAE's connection to India also supported the vested interests of the United States in the region. In fact, Washington was in favor of deeper engagement between India and the Middle East so that its growing interests and rising influence in the region would eventually turn the tide away from China.[153]

For this critical reason, the Emiratis were encouraged to boost their incipient ties with Japan, as another close American ally hailing from the East. At a time when the Japanese were building a proactive policy toward the wider Middle East in order to partially counterbalance China's growing clout, the UAE could play a constructive role by providing a platform for a larger Japanese presence in both the public and private sectors.[154]

---

[151] Kenneth Katzman, "United Arab Emirates (UAE): Issues for U.S. Policy," (Washington, D.C.: Congressional Research Service Report for Congress, June 23, 2010), pp. 8–9.

[152] Such crucial development was taking place in spite of the UAE's allegedly extensive lobbying measures, sometimes clandestinely, in the United States and in some other powerful European capitals in order to safeguard its rising stakes here and there. For more details, see: "What are the Limits of Foreign Lobbying in the UK?" *Al Jazeera*, July 18, 2018.

[153] "The Sprouting of the 'Look West' Policy," *The Hindu*, August 19, 2015.

[154] "Japan in Talks to Export Defense Aircraft to UAE," *Nikkei Asian Review*, August 27, 2017; and "Japan and UAE Agree to Expand Cooperation during Abe's Visit," *The Japan Times*, May 1, 2018.

South Korea was another Asian ally of the United States with which the UAE developed unprecedented political, economic, and military rela-tions. No aspect of such bilateral areas of partnership between Abu Dhabi and Seoul turned out to be more controversial than an undisclosed military deal the two sides signed in the wake of their groundbreaking nuclear power plant deal agreed in 2009. Since January 2011, as a consequence of that secret military pact, the Republic of Korea (ROK) dispatched, on a rotational basis, hundreds of its elite armed forces to the UAE in order to conduct joint mili-tary exercises and engage in exchanges with their Emirati counterparts. What particularly triggered debates in South Korea was a special clause in the military deal which specified that it did not require any approval by the Korean National Assembly.[155] The situation was particularly exacerbated when the Arab country later entered the Yemeni military civil war, making many people in the ROK anxious that their military forces stationed in the UAE might be ultimately and gratuitously dragged into another internecine conflict in the Middle East.[156]

Meanwhile, the UAE reached out to those whom Washington consid-ered its adversaries in East Asia as well: North Korea and particularly China. Their contacts with Pyongyang were mainly related to covert military deals, though the Emiratis also gave other timely economic boons to the commu-nist regime by opening part of their bustling construction market to North Korea's laborers with their work-hardened hands. It's important to note that the UAE's military bargaining with the Democratic People's Republic of Korea (DPRK) preceded its looking-East orientation, harkening back to the late 1980s when the Arab country kept its Western allies in the dark while purchasing Scud-B missiles from the communist regime of Kim Il-sung.

In 2015, moreover, it was reported that the UAE had brought in another cargo of munitions from North Korea, primarily for their military campaign in Yemen.[157] After all, the UAE's latest arms procurement from Pyongyang sharply contradicted Abu Dhabi's blunt anti-DPRK diplomatic rhetoric in the midst of another international political campaign supported by the Emiratis to oppose the United States, and other powerful members of the 5+1

---

[155] "Ex-South Korean Defense Minister Reveals Secret Seoul Defense Pact with UAE," *Asia Times*, January 10, 2018; and "Risky Business: South Korea's Secret Military Deal with UAE," *The Diplomat*, March 1, 2018.

[156] In fact, many Korean citizens still had a vivid memory of the Iraq War of 2003 during which the dispatch of South Korean military forces to the war-torn Middle Eastern country met with huge nation-wide demonstrations and anti-war campaigns, though the ROK forces apparently did not engage in any highly unpredictable and life-threatening operation during the course of their Iraqi mission. "S. Korean Special Forces in UAE a 'Trip Wire' in Yemini Civil War: Lawmaker," *Korea Herald*, September 6, 2018.

[157] "Why did the UAE Purchase Weapons from North Korea?" *The Diplomat*, August 8, 2017.

group, for engaging in serious negotiations to settle the international controversy over the Iranian nuclear program.

In comparison to North Korea, however, China stood out as a focal point of the UAE's looking-East push. The two countries had established official diplomatic ties in November 1984 and later exchanged first visits by their heads of state in 1989 and 1990.[158] By 2012, the Chinese and Emirati leaders could reach the pinnacle of their bilateral relationship as exemplified by concluding a major strategic partnership between the two countries. The UAE strived to position itself as a pivotal partner for Chinese regional ambitions in the Middle East and especially in the Persian Gulf region.[159] In order to maximize its benefit from China's rising status in the region, the tiny Arab state was keenly interested in becoming a major station serving China's newly developing maritime Silk Road. The Emiratis even allocated part of their lavish defense budget to purchasing arms and sensitive military equipment such as drones from China, pointedly proving their willingness to curry favor with the Chinese. The perception was that the rising East Asian power could soon reciprocate such Emirati favoritism in other areas, ranging from buying more crude oil to selling certain other sought-after newfangled technologies not easily accessible from the Western markets.[160]

The staying power of energy exports: New dynamics

Before the discovery of oil in Abu Dhabi in 1958, the average inhabitants of what were at that time called the Trucial States (now collectively called the United Arab Emirates), were living a harsh lifestyle. In order to keep body and soul together, they had to do whatever they could, legitimately and illegitimately, ranging from fishing and operating a dwindling pearl industry on the one hand to piracy and looting on the other.

Once the black gold was discovered, a new era in the history of the land was ushered in, something beyond the dreams of anyone there. The ruling sheikhs of different parts of the territory called for independence from Britain as well as unification; a dream which was to be materialized on December

---

[158] Former Chinese president Yang Shangkun visited Abu Dhabi in 1989 and the then UAE ruler, Sheikh Zayed bin Sultan Al Nahyan, paid back the visit by traveling to Beijing in 1990.

[159] "How Ties with China Bolster the UAE's Bid for Regional Dominance," *Middle East Eye*, August 12, 2019.

[160] "Is the UAE Secretly Buying Chinese Killer Drones?" *The diplomat*, January 30, 2018; "China, UAE to Expand Defence Industry Ties," *IHS Markit*, July 23, 2018; and "Ambitious UAE Flexes Military Muscle," *Reuters*, August 27, 2018.

2, 1971.[161] From then on, oil became the fountainhead of all economic and social changes the Emiratis were to experience. The UAE began to undergo a tectonic transformation, particularly in the aftermath of the oil shocks in 1973 and 1979, but nearly all the changes were underwritten by petrodollars. In the space of just two decades, therefore, the power of oil revenues re-wove the entire warp and woof of the UAE economy just as it revolutionized the socio-cultural patterns of its ordinary citizens.

Oil revenue made it possible for the UAE to develop an array of disparate economic activities, from expanding their ports to building headline-grabbing artificial islands and creating sparkling new financial and commercial centers. This earned the country the honor of "the most diversified economy" in the GCC. The Emiratis could move away from a strictly oil-based economy by placing more reliance on business and service sectors. In spite of achieving significance progress in economic diversification over time, however, energy revenues still play a critical role in the management of state affairs in the UAE. In fact, the bulk of the state budget is financed by the incomes the country makes through selling oil and natural gas. True, in Dubai oil makes up only a tiny percentage of the economy, but in the other six emirates of the federation the same cannot be said. Visitors to Dubai might not find an atmosphere suggestive of an oil town, but for the time being oil does function like a glue binding together the seven constituent emirates of the UAE. More than 90 percent of the country's oil flows from Abu Dhabi, the largest emirate and home of the UAE's political capital.[162] The tiny Arab country is home to the world's seventh and seventeenth largest reserves of oil and natural gas, respectively, making the issue of securing sustainable energy exports a priority.

As a consequence oil, and generally the shipment of energy sources, have been the mainstay of the UAE's looking-East program. The insatiable thirst of giant oil consumers in Asia can fund both the process of economic diversification at home and the diversification of export markets abroad. The Emiratis also wish to eventually upend the tradition of Western dominance over their oil industry. Thus, the UAE gradually smoothed the way for more oil companies from Asian countries to participate in its oil and natural gas industries.[163] Through bilateral contracts, Asian energy corporations have been awarded multiple stakes in the UAE's oil and natural gas projects which

---

[161] Ronald Codrai, *The Seven Sheikhdoms: Life in the Trucial States before the Federation of the United Arab Emirates* (London: Stacey International, 1990), pp. 12–13.

[162] Christopher M. Davidson, *Abu Dhabi: Oil and Beyond* (London: Hurst & Company, 2009), p. 69.

[163] George Eberling, *Chinese Energy Futures and Their Implications for the United States* (Lanham, MD: Lexington Books, 2011), p. 60.

once had been considered a prerogative of Western companies. Because of their financial power and technological capability, companies from Japan, South Korea and China have been particularly big winners of several lucrative energy contracts awarded by the Emiratis.[164]

Over time, Asian countries emerged as major importers of the UAE's oil and natural gas. The UAE became the second largest country in the GCC after Saudi Arabia to supply crude oil to Japan.[165] In fact, the Japanese import about one quarter of their oil from the Emiratis. Under long-term supply arrangements, moreover, the UAE has become a major exporter of liquefied petroleum gas to the East Asian country, though the Arab state itself is an importer of natural gas from the neighboring country of Qatar.[166]

Besides Japan, China has surfaced as another major stakeholder and oil-hungry behemoth for the UAE's energy exports. After China became a net importer of oil products in 1993 and a net importer of crude oil in 1996, its share of the UAE's petroleum exports significantly increased one year after another. During the second half of the 1990s and in the 2000s, the Emiratis came out as the second biggest supplier of oil to China in the GCC after Saudi Arabia. The UAE is still one of the top 15 suppliers of crude oil to China, selling them some $4 billion worth of petroleum in 2017.[167]

Meanwhile, the Emirati oil was used as a partial replacement for Iranian crude exports, which were shrinking due to the anti-Iran sanctions imposed by the West. The United States requested both Saudi Arabia and the UAE to ship more crude oil to a number of major oil consumers in Asia.[168] This measure was critical in order to seek the cooperation of China and others regarding the sanctions levied against the Iranians.[169] Like some of their counterparts in the GCC, the Emiratis had also expressed their willingness to take care of the energy requirements of some influential Asian nations, China in particular, if those countries were prepared to put additional politico-economic and financial pressure on Iran by committing themselves to the sanctions regime.[170] More importantly, the UAE's intermediary

[164] "Japan Takes another Stab at Renewing Abu Dhabi Oil Concessions," *Nikkei Asian Review*, February 2, 2018; and "UAE Awards Key Contracts to Samsung," *Hurriyet Daily News*, March 26, 2018.

[165] "Japan Set to Halt Imports of Iranian Oil," *Nikkei Asian Review*, July 19, 2018.

[166] "Japanese Prime Minister Praises Relations with Oil-rich UAE," *The Seattle Times*, April 30, 2018.

[167] "China Remains Dubai's Biggest Trade Partner in H1," *Xinhua*, September 19, 2018.

[168] Øystein Tunsjø, *Security and Profit in China's Energy Policy: Hedging against Risk* (New York: Columbia University Press, 2013), p. 104.

[169] "Japan's Cosmo Oil Replaces Iran Oil with other Mideast Supplies," *Reuters*, September 23, 2018.

[170] "Saudi, UAE Ready to Press China on Iran Sanctions: US," *France 24*, March 11, 2010; and Katzman, p. 9.

commercial role buttressed by its location close to Iran's southern coastlines was helpful in smoothing the way for the East's effective participation in the US-led international sanctions imposed on the Iranians.

Entrepôt trade: A sprouting maritime nexus

A great deal of the UAE's present-day prosperity and enviable regional standing has to do with the robust success of its metropolis city, Dubai, which has positioned itself as one of the world's busiest ports and a hub of intraregional connectivity. Dubai has played a critical role in facilitating trade links between the Persian Gulf region and the rest of the world, Asia in particular, over the past several decades, though both the pearl and oil industries had paved the way for such an eventuality.[171] In spite of a long history of trade and commercial interactions between the region and other parts of Asia, however, the rise of Dubai is largely due to a specific set of circumstances which had little to do with the policies and performances of the Emiratis themselves. Many other port cities around Dubai certainly had better potential and greater capabilities in terms of bringing an important component of globalization to the region or serving as a bridge to connect a whole host of neighboring countries and territories to other parts of the world.[172]

Once the UAE was tasked with putting up modern infrastructures and maritime logistic capacities, therefore, Dubai's Jebel Ali port emerged ultimately as an inter-regional trading and re-export hub, connecting Asian countries to the Middle East, North Africa, and Europe. Today, most of the UAE's largest trading partners are from Asia. A number of Asian countries like Japan and South Korea have established significant non-oil trade with the UAE, a bulk of which is handled through the Dubai entrepôt. More importantly, China and India have become Dubai's first and second biggest trading partners, respectively. In 2017, the total value of the Chinese trade with the Arab country reached around $52 billion, 52 percent of which took place between the UAE's free zones and the East Asian country.[173] Of the entire Middle East region, Dubai has also become the largest trading partner of China's Hong Kong. In the same way, the UAE accounted for some two-thirds of India's exports to the entire GCC region by the year 2000. A decade later, still more than half of India's total trade with the GCC took place

---

[171] Michael Quentin Morton, *Keepers of the Golden Shore: A History of the United Arab Emirates* (London: Reaktion Books Ltd, 2016).
[172] Miller, p. 288.
[173] "UAE–China Trade Hits 52.65 bln USD in 2017," *Xinhua*, July 5, 2018; and "Dubai Becomes Transshipment Point as China–Mideast Trade Flourishes," *Global Times*, June 24, 2019.

between the South Asian country and the UAE. The Indian–UAE commercial interactions are expected to hit more than $100 billion by 2020.[174]

The bright prospect of the rising Eastern powers' expanding commercial relationship with the region has galvanized the Dubai authorities to
double down on their Asia-oriented policies and measures *pari passu* with the
Arab country's looking-East drive. As a case in point, Dubai Ports World, an
important company owned by the government of Dubai, has invested heavily
in a string of Chinese coastal cities, operating container terminals in major
port cities like Hong Kong.[175] The Chinese government has equally played an
instrumental role in laying the groundwork for a larger presence of Dubai in
China's international ports. After all, China wants to place the UAE as a key
node in its "Belt and Road" initiatives, turning Dubai into a beachhead for its
growing commercial connections to the wider Middle East and beyond. The
entrepôt function of Dubai would become even more vital to the Chinese
if the United States and China show themselves to be serious in launching
retaliatory trade wars against each other.[176]

The "beating heart" of a barren desert: Becoming a financial hub

For more than a decade, the UAE has strived to establish itself as a credible financial hub, regionally and even internationally, by taking advantage
of its financial and geographic assets. The tiny state is actually among the
world's largest holders of sovereign wealth funds (SWFs), on a par with
countries like Norway, Russia, China, Saudi Arabia, and Kuwait. Abu Dhabi's
SWF is estimated to be around $1 trillion. This enormous financial muscle
is further empowered by Dubai's critical role in facilitating massive international flows and interconnectedness, buoying up the Emiratis, creating a
conducive environment for many foreign banks and financial institutions to
operate on their sovereign territory.[177] With an initial emphasis on private
banking and asset management, since the early 2000s the UAE has enacted

---

[174] "Dubai Named among World's Top 5 Shipping Hubs," *Arabian Business*, July 28, 2018; and
"Dubai Targets Hong Kong as Part of Far East Exports Push," *Arabian Business*, August 15,
2018.

[175] Christopher M. Davidson, *After the Sheikhs: The Coming Collapse of the Gulf Monarchies* (New
York: Oxford University Press, 2013), p. 108.

[176] "Trade War Likely to Usher World into Chaos," *Global Times*, July 3, 2018; and "The US
Sees the Trade War as a Tactic to Contain China. So Does Beijing," *South China Morning
Post*, July 4, 2018.

[177] Because of such advantages, the UAE cities, Dubai in particular, have also been exploited
to launder money by many international criminals of every persuasion, including war
profiteers, terror financers, drugs smugglers, and human traffickers. For more details, see:
"Dubai to Hong Kong, Follow the Money (Laundering)," *South China Morning Post*, August
5, 2018.

---

new rules and regulations to expand its role.[178] To entice international banks and investment funds, the Emiratis have particularly relaxed the rules for business ownership and permanent residency in addition to offering low taxes.[179]

In order to achieve their long-term objective of rivaling financial centers such as London and New York, the UAE cities of Dubai and Abu Dhabi inevitably tapped into the sprouting financial resources of the rising Asian powers and jumped on the bandwagon of looking East.[180] In January 2012, the Emiratis and their Chinese counterparts signed an agreement on bilateral currency swaps. This smoothed the way for the two countries to launch a joint investment cooperation fund in 2015 with each party contributing an initial capital injection of $5 billion. In July 2018, moreover, China and the UAE announced the inception of the first Chinese state-owned financial services firm to be established in Abu Dhabi Global Market (ADGM), which is essentially the financial nucleus of the political capital.[181] The ADGM had already announced the launch of its first overseas representative office in Beijing in May 2018.[182] As a consequence of such bilateral initiatives, the Chinese banks and financial institutions now make up roughly a quarter of all assets booked in Dubai International Financial Center (DIFC).[183]

In the wake of the worldwide financial crisis of 2007–2008, however, the success of Dubai and Abu Dhabi raised questions in some other financial cities that worried about their future. Hong Kong rushed to sign a cooperation agreement with Abu Dhabi to jointly support and promote financial services, while the Singaporean financial institutions looked with concern on Dubai and Abu Dhabi's surprising encroachment on their own international standing.[184] In the same way, some countries in the region such as Qatar and Turkey were envious of the Emiratis' financial prospects, and they set out to identify a number of financial policies and market strategies that might enable them one day to compete comfortably with Dubai and Abu

---

[178] International Monetary Fund, *United Arab Emirates: Financial System Stability Assessment* (Washington, D.C.: International Monetary Fund, 2007), p. 13; and Miller, p. 288.

[179] "New UAE Visa Law Might Propel it to Top 10 World Financial Hubs," *Albawaba*, September 18, 2018.

[180] "UAE Strives to Become Financial Innovation Center, Taking Advantage of China's B&R Initiative," *Xinhua*, May 27, 2018.

[181] "China and UAE Sign Oil, Trade and Financial Agreements," *Al Arabiya*, July 20, 2018.

[182] "Abu Dhabi's Financial Hub Launches First Office in China," *Arabia Business*, May 25, 2018.

[183] "Revealed: How China is Driving Growth in Dubai's Financial Hub," *Arabian Business*, May 16, 2018; and "Dubai Turning Strategic Hub for Chinese Investors," *China Daily*, February 13, 2019.

[184] "Will Abu Dhabi's Finance Hub Eat Singapore's Lunch?" *The Straits Times*, November 11, 2015.

Dhabi.[185] All that notwithstanding, many Asian banks and financial institutions have so far demonstrated a keen interest to foster closer financial cooperation with and connections to the Emiratis. One pivotal reason is the UAE's overall role in smoothing the path of Asian commercial ties with Iran.

Drawbridge: Linking Iran and the East

For all the strident rhetoric and tough talk on Iran in certain parts, the UAE for decades has played an indispensable role in greasing the wheels of the Islamic Republic's international commercial juggernaut. Given its international political isolation, a quasi-economic autarky, and a sundry of universal sanctions levied against Iran, the Islamic Republic could not really make ends meet without taking advantage of places like Dubai as a major commercial hub and shipping route. This opportunity has helped it to manage its massive business deals with other parts of the world, East Asia in particular.

A slew of Iranian companies were registered in Dubai and the city itself became a new home for a large community of Iranian citizens, many of whom engaged in commercial interactions with the East.[186] As a corollary to that, commercial ties between the UAE and Iran leaped from strength to strength one year after another. The two sides often fussed over politico-strategic grievances but without airing any meaningful complaint with regard to their bustling economic relationship.[187]

The UAE was looking to expand its economic interests in general, while Iran was making the most of its small Arab neighbor by finding ways, particularly through Dubai, to keep its commercial links to Asia uninterrupted. Because of this, some interested observers accused the Emiratis of assisting the Iranians evading US-led economic sanctions — even at the times when Iran was only bartering Asian products for crude oil, which it was supplying to the East via the UAE ports. Some commentators tried to blame the UAE for the partial failure of the sanctions regime (legal or not) imposed against Tehran, because the Emiratis had made it possible for Iran to skirt the sanctions through fostering numerous Dubai-based connections to many Asian countries and some other parts of the world. The Emiratis were even held accountable for paving the way for the sale of some highly sensitive items,

---

[185] "Qatar Sets Aside $2 Billion in Bid to Rival Dubai Financial Hub," *Bloomberg*, October 8, 2018.

[186] Benjamin B. Smith, *Hard Times in the Lands of Plenty: Oil Politics in Iran and Indonesia* (Ithaca, NY: Cornell University Press, 2007), p. 164.

[187] Katzman, p. 9.

including nuclear technologies, to Iran via the UAE.[188] Whether or not such harsh accusations could hold water, the UAE did become very instrumental in assisting the progress of Iran's imports and exports with the East.

Regarding imports, Iran had to rely on the UAE for bringing in a great deal of its industrial and consumer requirements. The Emiratis themselves were obviously not producing such stuff; they were serving as a go-between in transporting many types of goods from Asia and other regions to Iran. In fact, the UAE emerged as a primary destination in the Middle East for a whole host of Asian products, a large percentage of which was to be re-exported to Iran.[189] The tiny Arab entrepôt became either the first or the second top trading partner of many Eastern countries, including China, Japan, South Korea, Taiwan, Singapore, etc. Iran was the main factor in this, since its bustling market of some 80 million consumers was heavily dependent on imported goods — mostly produced somewhere in Asia.[190] Iran's problems had indubitably been compounded by international sanctions and other technical restrictions, but the intermediary function of the UAE in channeling Asian products into the country did not change much once Tehran signed the nuclear deal and a brief normalization in its international relations ensued.[191]

In the same way, the UAE turned out to be among the top destinations for most of Iran's non-oil exports, though the Emiratis were also importing from Iran large amounts of energy products such as condensates. The small population of the UAE, with convenient access to any type of foreign commodity, was not itself a major consumer of such products. A significant volume of those goods were to be repackaged and then re-exported to Asia and other regions.[192] More importantly, when the Iranian oil industry came under bouts of international sanctions, Tehran had to rely more on its non-oil exports as a major source of foreign currency to meet its growing domestic needs. Since some of Iran's major partners in the East were either unwilling or unable to purchase Iran's non-oil goods directly, the UAE was often the only option through which the two sides could strike a business deal.[193]

---

[188] Bryan R. Early, *Busted Sanctions: Explaining Why Economic Sanctions Fail* (Stanford, CA: Stanford University Press, 2015), p. 88–89.

[189] Peter Cooper, *Opportunity Dubai: Making a Fortune in the Middle East* (Hampshire, UK: Harriman House LTD, 2008), pp. 34, 176.

[190] "How Dubai Has Benefited from Regional Turmoil, from the Kuwait Invasion to the War on Terror," *CNBC*, October 29, 2018.

[191] "Pompeo Talks Tough on Iran While Visiting the Emirates," *Daily Herald*, July 10, 2018.

[192] "Dubai's Non-oil Trade with South Korea Rises to $7.4bn," *Arabian Business*, March 26, 2018.

[193] "Iran Oil Buyer and Rival, U.A.E., May be Cracking Down on Trade," *Bloomberg*, October 3, 2018.

The construction connection: Excelsior with Asians

In the wake of the first and second oil shocks, when the prices of crude oil ratcheted up astonishingly to around $12 and $35 per barrel, respectively, the UAE like some of its energy-rich counterparts allocated a wad of hard cash for a wide-ranging array of construction projects.[194] This was the beginning of an unprecedented, zealous quest to build a different identity by transforming the architectural landscape of the desert federation. And it was no passing infatuation. A decades-long building craze expressed an endless devotion to creation and expansion, through setting up high-priced edifices and carrying out expensive infrastructure projects. Impressive skyscrapers were erected, lofty towers were put up, and dazzling artificial islands became the hallmarks of a modern and trendsetting UAE. The East had certainly contributed greatly to these superlative achievements, and its anticipated rise could only further excite the thirst of the Emiratis.

In particular, over the past decade the UAE has engaged in new areas of construction cooperation with Asian countries. A turning point came in December 2009 when the Emiratis signed a contract with a South Korean consortium led by the Korean Electronic Power Company (KEPCO) to construct four nuclear plants. The sweet deal, valued $18.6 billion, was meant to further reduce the wealthy UAE's reliance on fossil fuels by tapping into new sources of clean energy.[195] In March 2018, a large crowd of Emirati and Korean officials gathered at the Barakah power plant to celebrate the completion of the first nuclear reactor, which was built for the UAE by the Koreans to one day make the Arab country an exporter of nuclear energy.[196] Moreover, the UAE and Chinese governments later started serious talks about collaborating on a whole host of infrastructure and renewable energy projects. As part of its ambitious Belt and Road Initiative, China singled out the UAE as a proper venue for the construction of an interconnected system of maritime, railways, roads, and other transport facilities which could considerably elevate the position and standing of the Arab entrepôt in the region.[197]

---

[194] Sean Hickey, *Confessions of an International Banker* (Bloomington, IN: Trafford Publishing, 2013), p. 162.

[195] "South Korea's KEPCO Shortlisted to Bid for Saudi Nuclear Project," *Reuters*, July 1, 2018; and "S. Korea Seeks Partnership with US, UAE to Win Saudi Arabia's Power Plant Orders," *KBS*, July 3, 2018.

[196] "South Korea to Help UAE Become Nuclear Exporter," *Nikkei Asian Review*, March 27, 2018; and "UAE and South Korea Celebrate Completion of Barakah's First Nuclear Reactor," *The National*, March 26, 2018.

[197] "Carry out the Silk Road Spirit, and Deepen China–Arab State Cooperation," *People's Daily*, June 5, 2014, p. A1; and "An Opportunity for China and UAE to Meet on Silk Road," *Gulf News*, April 8, 2015.

After making significant deals with South Korea and China, the UAE continued looking East, courting India and Japan for a number of perhaps even more ambitious projects. As a case in point, the Emiratis and Indians discussed the feasibility of a 2000 km undersea rail line to transport both people and goods between India and the UAE via high-speed floating trains. If materialized, such a novel project would fundamentally and permanently transform the nature and scope of the UAE's connections to the world.

With regard to Japan, the Emiratis want to take advantage of Japanese expertise and technical knowhow since they sent a probe to Mars in July 2020. Under an equally adventurous plan, they intend to exploit Japanese experience and skills to construct a science city on Mars within the century.[198] It seems that by comparison to the UAE's aspirations for future construction, the glittering towers of the 80s and 90s are nothing but humdrum office blocks.

Meanwhile, Asian workers, a major component of the UAE's construction industry, are expected to play a more visible role in the newly-launched projects. Some 20 million or roughly 40 percent of the entire population of the GGC countries are foreign workers, mostly from South and Southeast Asia as well as from Africa. Of these, the UAE hosts the largest number; and it is also the fifth biggest recipient of foreign workers in the world. These workers account for more than three quarters of the entire UAE's population, while over 50 percent of the country's current inhabitants are workers from Asian countries, including India, Pakistan, Bangladesh, Sri Lanka, Nepal, the Philippines, and Thailand.[199] Of course, not all of these Asian workers are hired to labor for contractors, but they are the backbone of any construction project contracted for the UAE. A great number of the UAE's elephantine projects, including Burj Khalifa (formerly Burj Dubai), have been erected by the hard work of Asian laborers.[200]

The large presence of Asian workers in the UAE has, however, never been devoid of controversy. For instance, the UAE has reportedly allowed the recruitment of a good number of North Korean laborers, to work mostly on construction sites.[201] It is alleged that these pitiable manual laborers, like their fellow citizens working in other GCC states, have benefited the

---

[198] "Rocket Carrying 1st UAE-made Satellite Launched from Japan," *The Washington Post*, October 29, 2018.

[199] Jim Krane, *Dubai: The Story of the World's Fastest City* (New York: St Martin's Press, 2009); and Miller, p. 225.

[200] Michael Herb, *The Wages of Oil: Parliaments and Economic Development in Kuwait and the UAE* (New York: Cornell University Press, 2014), p. 114.

[201] "UAE to Stop Issuing Visas to North Koreans," *Voice of America*, October 12, 2017.

communist regime of Pyongyang instead of primarily helping themselves and their own family members.[202]

Moreover, many workers in the UAE (and other GCC countries) have reportedly been subject to various types of mental, physical, and wage abuses. In a country where trade unions are not permitted to exist and workers have absolutely no rights, a foreign "guest worker" from a poor country is certainly a sitting duck.[203] But the Emiratis prefer to hire Asian workers more than laborers from other Arab nations and Africa. A major reason is that Asians are more segregated, less interested in applying for permanent residency, and thereby pose little threat to the cultural complexion and recent prosperity of the indigenous Emirati population in the long haul.

Creating cultural magnetism

After decades of development and material betterment, the UAE cities, Dubai in particular, have gradually emerged as a role model across the Middle East and beyond. It can demonstrate its modern achievements and distinction in worldly aspects as well as in the intangible realm. The blazing lights of Dubai have made it the top tourist attraction in the Middle East and a major international destination, including for well-heeled Asian visitors.[204] Moreover, this metropolis is now one of the most popular places in the world for expats to work and live, as the city makes it possible for many foreign professionals and talented experts to earn relatively high wages and various other perks. The entertainment industry of the city has flourished over the years, too, as divers options for amusement and recreation proliferate. Even those people who have developed a refined taste in intellectual activities are increasingly finding new venues and opportunities across the UAE to fulfil their own interests and expectations.

As part of their looking-East drive, therefore, the Emiratis perceived a rising East to be a new engine to empower their cultural capacities in the same way they are enhancing their material well-beings. Much the same as

---

[202] This is certainly not the case with regard to other Asian laborers working in the GCC countries. For instance, it is estimated that roughly $14 billion, or more than one-fourth of India's combined remittances, flows from its citizens working across the GCC region.

[203] Human Rights Watch, *"The Island of Happiness": Exploitation of Migrant Workers on Saadiyat Island, Abu Dhabi* (New York: Human Rights Watch, 2009), p. 2.

[204] In 2017, for instance, more than one million Chinese nationals visited the UAE. More than half of them (54 percent) went there for leisure purposes and some one-third (33 percent) only for business. In 2018, some 875,000 Chinese nationals visited Dubai alone, enabling China to climb to fourth spot after India, Saudi Arabia, and Britain, respectively. "One-third of Chinese Travellers to UAE Visit for Business," *Arabian Business*, August 5, 2018; and "Chinese Tourists to Dubai up 12 pct in 2018: Report," *Xinhua*, February 24, 2019.

the UAE's largest commercial airlines, Emirates and Etihad Airways, looked to Asian countries for new business and growth opportunities, the country's cultural authorities realized that a new thriving Asia had the potential to significantly boost their soft power in the region.[205] If the UAE was previously a major destination for unskilled Asian laborers, it could now be a top choice for Asian talent, as experts can enjoy their professional work and a more comfortable lifestyle. And if many UAE officials were used to negotiating with their Asian counterparts about commerce and construction, they have now come to appreciate the role of cultural influence and so they find themselves approving educational and research collaboration with the East, in addition to hosting lots of other media and entertainment initiatives agreed between both sides.[206]

For their part, Asian countries have become cognizant of the necessity to foster stronger cultural ties to the UAE for the sake of consolidating their rising role in the region. Instead of focusing only on business contracts, many in Asia have now tried to build more connections to the UAE's local culture and community.[207] Some Asian nations relaxed their previous travel and visa restrictions for Emirati citizens, while other countries such as China and Japan exempted the UAE nationals from any visa requirement for tourism and short-term sojourns.[208] To better win over the Emiratis, South Koreans have promoted their *Hallyu* products through public outlets and private intermediaries,[209] while North Koreans have availed themselves of the opportunity to showcase their superlative art and cultural performances in the Arab country.[210] Japan has launched more retail markets across the UAE to promote its culture, and entrepreneurs from India have set up more Indian travel agencies and restaurants there. Additionally, people from Asian countries have been encouraged to travel to the UAE, turning some Eastern countries such as China into the fastest expanding source of tourists for the Arab country.[211]

---

[205] "Emirates Sees Growth from the East," *The National*, April 25, 2017.

[206] Davidson, *After the Sheikhs*, 109; and "UAE, China Sign Pact on TV Series Shows," *Khmer Times*, July 15, 2018.

[207] "Chinese Brands Shine at Dubai Fashion Event," *Xinhua*, November 26, 2018.

[208] "UAE Nationals to Get Visa-free Entry into Japan," *Arabian Business*, June 21, 2017; and "Visa-free Travel to China for UAE Nationals Begins," *The National*, January 16, 2018.

[209] "Mansour's Family Member Proposes to Korean Singer, Rumors say," *Korea Times*, January 17, 2016.

[210] "U.N.: North Korea Art Exhibit in UAE Could Violate Sanctions," *UPI*, April 11, 2018.

[211] "Dubai Tourism Industry Works to Lure Chinese," *Global Times*, July 18, 2018.

Conclusion

The capstone of the UAE's overall foreign and security objectives rests on maintaining close relationship with the powerful countries of the West, especially the United States of America. As a ramification of such a solid politico-strategic principle, the Emiratis also give high priority to keeping an ironclad alliance with a small set of like-minded fellow Arabs in the wider Middle East. Beyond this overarching proposition, the UAE's friendly political rhetoric and agreeable diplomatic gestures toward other countries and other regions seem to be more symbolic than substantive, aiming to essentially preserve and promote its non-politico-strategic interests. Abu Dhabi's recent proactive policy of looking East falls within this compass. The Emiratis have worked to forge multifaceted connections to many Asian countries, the rising powers of China and India in particular, with the hope of bolstering their own economic and financial interests in an emerging East.

The UAE certainly benefitted plenty from its earlier relations with Asia. For a couple of decades, the supply of crude oil to the industrializing and developing countries there brought back huge revenues with which the Emiratis could underwrite their massive infrastructure projects. Asian contractors as well as hordes of Asian manual laborers played an instrumental role in erecting the skyscrapers and carrying out many other monumental construction schemes across the UAE, especially in the metropolitan port city of Dubai. The Asian workforce also became a mainstay of the business and service sectors in the small GCC country. The looking-East orientation is, therefore, successfully enhancing the reputation and advantageous position of the UAE in the larger Middle East and beyond. For the Emiratis, the objective is to make the most of their current leverage in the region to rise even higher.

All in all, the UAE has some very good reasons to be confident about the rosy prospects of its ongoing looking-East push. For now, the commanding heights of international politics seem to favor the Emiratis and their present standing. Not only did the successful surge of the Emiratis within the Middle East come about because of a unique set of circumstances, which their arch rivals in the region can hardly hope to experience any time soon, it is also unlikely that the powerful non-regional stakeholders are really willing to turn their backs on the Arab entrepôt in the foreseeable future. Consequently, the UAE's expanding infrastructure as well as its massive foreign workforce (hailing largely from Asian countries) have contributed to its advantageous position as a connection point to the East. The rising

Asian powers are equally keen to make strides in every area favorable to their interests by capitalizing on the UAE's looking-East approach.

CHAPTER 4. IRAQ: PINNING HOPE ON THE EAST AFTER THE LET-DOWN BY THE WEST

Accused and invaded by the United States and its coalition partners for allegedly possessing weapons of mass destruction (WMDs), the ruined and ravaged Iraq was supposed to emerge eventually as a model of democracy and prosperity. According to the rhetoric of the time, the downtrodden Iraqi citizens were promised a free and flourishing society after being offered a unique chance to get rid of their authoritarian and prejudiced political system governed by Saddam Hussein's Ba'ath Party.[212] The whole idea, as declared many times by U.S. officials, was to ultimately turn the shattered Middle Eastern country into a thriving, Western-style politico-economic system, the way the highly successful German and Japanese societies were reorganized in the aftermath of World War II. The US-led West suggested that they could and would reproduce such awesome and impressive stories of nation-building and democratization, and furthermore would use post-Saddam Iraq as a blueprint for the transformation of the entire region.[213]

Despite those radiant prophecies, those stunning predictions never materialized. After the immediate mission of invasion and occupation, the country was plunged into a long period of catastrophic insurgency and civil war, teetering on the brink of total bankruptcy and disintegration. Ethnic disunity and political altercations replaced the critical task of nation-

---

[212] Marc Weller, *Iraq and the Use of Force in International Law* (New York: Oxford University Press, 2010), pp. 128, 132.
[213] Anton D. Lowenberg and Timothy Mathews, "Why Iraq?" *Defence and Peace Economics*, Vol. 19, No. 1 (2008), pp. 1–20.

building and progressive social transformation.[214] The Americans and their Western partners did not live up to their pledges to rebuild and reorganize the post-conflict Iraq. To add insult to injury, not only did the United States fail to play a leading role in refashioning the war-torn Iraqi state into a template of lasting stability and progress, it even refused to contribute any significant amount of capital and moral support to the reconstruction business and its advocates inside and outside the country.[215]

Ruined first and later shunned and disappointed by the West, therefore, post-war Iraq ineluctably had to turn to the East. For all the perennial domestic chaos and sharp divisions among the post-Saddam's ruling elites, Iraq desperately needed to demonstrate to the outside world that it was still a normal state with functioning structures and well-defined national objectives.[216] The country also needed a vast array of resources in order to muddle through against the backdrop of instability and confusion that was taking a great toll on its human and natural reserves.[217] Now that the Western countries, the United States in particular, were reluctant to actually help in the arduous task of Iraq's reconstruction and development,[218] the new Iraqi rulers found, out of the blue, some very resourceful partners in Asia willing to help in fulfilling those important goals.[219] What, then, did the Iraqi leaders wish to gain by making advances to the East, and what were the essential characteristics of their looking-East approach?

Soliciting Asian diggers: A new course of looking East

Post-war Iraq's orientation toward Asian countries was not really unprecedented in modern history, though there were some contrasts in the nature and scope of these approaches. For instance, an anti-monarchy coup d'état in Iraq in 1958 and the ensuing rise of the socialist Ba'ath Party in 1963 paved the ground for a close bilateral relationship between Baghdad and the communist regime of the DPRK. Their friendly ties were symbiotic and lasted, *mutatis mutandis*, until October 1980, when Saddam severed

---

[214] Andrew Parasiliti, "Leaving Iraq," *Survival*, Vol. 54, No. 1 (2012), pp. 127–133.

[215] "The Failed Reconstruction of Iraq," *The Atlantic*, March 15, 2013; and "US will not Contribute Cash at Iraq Reconstruction Conference: Report," *Middle East Eye*, February 9, 2018.

[216] Rolf Schwarz and Oliver Jütersonke, "Divisible Sovereignty and the Reconstruction of Iraq," *Third World Quarterly*, Vol. 26, No. 4–5 (2005), pp. 649–665; and "New Government in Iraq Courts Russian Embrace," *Asia Times*, December 13, 2018.

[217] Daniel Serwer, "Muddling Through in Iraq," *Survival*, Vol. 55, No. 4 (2013), pp. 35–40.

[218] "Allies Pledge Billions for Iraq's Reconstruction," *Reuters*, February 14, 2018.

[219] "Iraq's Oil Auction Hits the Jackpot," *Asia Times*, December 16, 2009; "Leading Newspaper Denies China's Exploitation of Iraq," *Xinhua*, August 13, 2014; and "Is China Wrong to Benefit from Iraq?" *People's Daily*, August 13, 2014.

all diplomatic connections to North Korea, accusing Pyongyang of having an allegiance to Iran. Thus it is no coincidence that on the cusp of the Iraq War the DPRK offered political asylum to Saddam and his family through a Hong Kong-based go-between, primarily in order to fend off an imminent military invasion by the United States against Baghdad.[220] Additionally, Saddam's Iraq had developed good relations, sometimes sporadic and stealthy, with a number of other Asian countries such as China, with which Baghdad engaged in significant military deals in the heyday of the Iran–Iraq War during the 1980s.[221]

Following the removal of Saddam and his Ba'ath Party from power, the new Iraqi leaders moved to gradually restore Baghdad's relations with almost all Asian countries, including North Korea. The general tenor of post-war Iraq's politics and economy also had a lot in common with Eastern rather than Western societies, compelling its neophyte rulers to cultivate better connections to Asian countries. The new looking-East orientation pursued by Baghdad, however, predominantly related to economic and technological requirements. Politically and culturally, the country leaned increasingly toward some of its neighboring countries.[222] Over time, the Iraqi leaders did demonstrate a willingness to forge multifaceted relations with their counterparts in the East, but meeting their own dire economic, financial, and technological needs certainly remained paramount — and the more successful Asian nations were seen as a potentially key element in this.[223]

Meanwhile, many Asian countries were equally eager to develop good ties with the post-Saddam Iraqi state. The previous regime of sundry sanctions against Iraq and its political isolation for many years had virtually blocked attempts by Asian countries to promote their interests in the Middle Eastern country. They had long been waiting in the wings for an opportunity to enter the resource-rich country, and the post-war openness of Iraq to the outside world provided them with just such a chance. Given its location, demographic size, and huge energy resources, Iraq was understood to have the potential to emerge eventually as a major prize. It was an alluring reward

---

[220] "Stanley Ho Claims North Korea Offered Dictator Asylum," *South China Morning Post*, March 2, 2003; and "Three Strange Links between Macau, North Korea: From Saddam Hussein to Customs Chief's Death," *South China Morning Post*, May 7, 2017.

[221] "Bilateral Relations between China and Iraq," *Embassy of the People's Republic of China in the Republic of Iraq*, April 11, 2013; and "China and Iraq Celebrate 60-year Relationship," *Kurdistan 24*, August 25, 2018.

[222] David Ghanim, *Iraq's Dysfunctional Democracy* (Santa Barbara, CA: Praeger, 2011), p. 199–201.

[223] "Iraqi Leader Eyes Japanese Model for Postwar Development," *The Asahi Shimbun*, April 11, 2018.

for any interested foreign investor and creditor.[224] As it turned out, Asian instead of Western countries showed more willingness and guts to throw their financial and technological resources into the chaotic scene, which was to remain, for many years to come, in the throes of terror, insurgency and civil strife.[225] As a corollary to that, the new Iraqi leaders were predisposed to broaden the scope of their looking-East drive in order to cover practically all political, military, economic, financial, technological, and even cultural spheres.[226]

Swift politico-diplomatic rapprochement and more perks

The Iraq War turned out to be one of the greatest catastrophes of all time. This precipitous adventure ultimately cost hundreds thousands of lives and hundreds of billions of dollars. The calamitous conflict also wreaked havoc on the reputation of the West and precipitated the decline of the hegemonic power of the United States in the international system.[227]

After more than one and half decades, there is still an incessant stream of academic publications and policy reports which continuously flail about trying to come up with a persuasive rationale for the war instigated by the George W. Bush administration in 2003.[228] The masterminds behind the war project certainly did not walk into that mortal trap on a whim, and there must have been some pivotal political, strategic or economic interests at stake to warrant such a reckless military action. But the neoconservative coterie of war in Washington and their close associates in London preferred not to explain their real motives to the inquisitive audience around the world, keeping many people guessing and others condemning the Western countries for their illegal action against Iraq.

In contrast to the Iraq War's ruinous ramifications for the West, the East came out of the cataclysmic conflict almost unscathed. Some Eastern countries even got credit for their "positive contribution" to the end result, while the war's architects and backers in the West were constantly condemned and chastised.

---

[224] Daniel Egan, "Globalization and the Invasion of Iraq: State Power and the Enforcement of Neoliberalism," *Sociological Focus*, Vol. 40, No. 1 (2007), pp. 98–111.

[225] Thomas S. Mowle, "Iraq's Militia Problem," *Survival*, Vol. 48, No. 3 (2006), pp. 41–58; and Phil Williams, "Organized Crime and Corruption in Iraq," *International Peacekeeping*, Vol. 16, No. 1 (2009), pp. 115–135.

[226] "Iraq's Future," *Strategic Comments*, Vol. 1, No. 8 (1995), pp. 1–2.

[227] Edward Luce, *The Retreat of Western Liberalism* (New York: Atlantic Monthly Press, 2017).

[228] "Bush's Recklessness, Obama's Fecklessness Leave U.S. Looking Weak as Iraq Crumbles," *The Baltimore Sun*, June 17, 2014.

In so far as Iraq's relationship with the outside world is concerned, the post-Saddam ruling elites played an instrumental role in meting out such rewards and rebukes. Suspicious and cynical public opinion inside and outside the country about the disastrous war often convinced the new Iraqi rulers to neither justify the West's action widely nor to praise its culprits publicly.[229] In comparison, they were often generous in highlighting the "helpful assistance" of Eastern nations to the new Iraq, using this to further improve Baghdad's relationship with one or other Asian country. By and large, the new rulers of Iraq found such a sanguine attitude about the role of Eastern countries in the outcome and the flattering remarks to be a good strategy to persuade more Asian countries to consider closer cooperation with their war-torn country.[230]

In fact, many rich and powerful Asian countries played a part in the Iraqi War which could later have warranted praise by the post-Saddam pro-US political leaders. Some were actively involved in the US-led campaign of 2003 against Baghdad, while staying out of it was all some other Eastern countries needed to do in order to secure their long-term national interests in the post-Saddam's Iraq.

The Japanese and South Korean governments emerged among the staunchest supporters of the Western alliance against Iraq, launching a great PR campaign at home to neutralize the negativity of their own down-beat and anti-war citizens in addition to vocally supporting the US-led military action against the Saddam regime.[231] Japan even moved against its own "peace constitution" by dispatching the country's Self-Defense Forces (SDFs) to the warzone; a highly perilous action soon followed by South Korea, though both East Asian countries declared unequivocally that their military forces had been sent to the safer parts of Iraq in order to engage in a "humanitarian mission" there.[232] It was then no coincidence that the post-war Iraqi leaders regularly heaped praise on the Japanese and Korean deeds

---

[229] A good number of Iraq's new ruling class were previously deadwood and nonentities whom the "Operation Iraqi Freedom" of 2003 catapulted into power and wealth overnight. Many of these scatterbrained opportunists and scheming potentates knew full well about the *fons et origo* of their instantaneous authority and inconceivable prosperity in the post-Saddam era, but they often looked the other way, talking and behaving as if they had climbed to power quite naturally through the legitimate ballot boxes of an organic and mature democratic system.

[230] "After the Iraq War: The View from Asia," *The Brookings Institution*, April 16, 2003; and "America Has Spent $5.9 Trillion on Wars in the Middle East and Asia since 2001, a New Study Says," *CNBC*, November 14, 2018.

[231] Shirzad Azad, "Japan's Gulf Policy and Response to the Iraq War," *The Middle East Review of International Affairs*, Vol. 12, No. 2 (June 2008) pp. 52–64.

[232] Michael Penn, *Japan and the War on Terror: Military Force and Political Pressure in the US-Japanese Alliance* (London and New York: I.B. Tauris, 2014), p. 120; "Abe Unveils Initiative to Boost Security in Iraq amid Arms Proliferation," *The Japan Times*, April 6, 2018; and "SDF

during the conflict, besides smoothing the way for closer politico-economic relations between the two sides in the long run.[233]

China was another Asian nation which eventually turned out to be a major winner of the Iraq War, in spite of the fact that it played an ambiguous role throughout the conflict. When the US-led military campaign broke out, the Chinese initially joined Russia, France and Germany in symbolically condemning the move. But they soon adjusted their position, without providing any explicit criticism of the Americans and their war coalition.[234] More importantly, China refrained from standing in the way of UN action and took several important measures domestically to mitigate public opposition against the military conflict in the Middle East. Once the major course of the military action was over, however, the Chinese managed to swiftly stabilize their relationship with Iraq by opening their Baghdad embassy in July 2004 and investing heavily in the country soon after. China's subsequent activities redounded greatly to its reputation and credibility in Iraq, making it possible for the two countries to elevate their growing interactions to "strategic partnership" in 2015.[235]

The last but not least important Eastern power in this equation was India which, like China, emerged as a big beneficiary of the Western attack against Saddam. The Indian government followed a so-called "middle path" during the conflict: the Indians neither threw their explicit support behind the US-led coalition nor did they get up on their soapbox denouncing the operation to topple the Ba'ath Party from power. Given India's previous record in the Non-Aligned Movement (NAM) and its advocacy of safeguarding international law, their approach was dubbed by some observers as an opportunistically "devious act" in favor of the United States.[236] Still, India's official position toward the war was later praised by the new Iraqi leadership, speeding up the process of normalizing diplomatic relations between the two countries. Like other Asians, Indians from the public and private sectors were also encouraged to pour their financial and technical resources into up-and-coming sectors in Iraq.

Logs on Iraq Mission Contain Several References to 'Combat': Defense Official," *The Japan Times*, April 14, 2018.

[233] Interestingly, Japan was among the first countries which started promoting the idea of "strategic partnership" with Iraq in 2007. "Is There a Japan–Iraq Strategic Partnership?" *Japan Focus*, November 3, 2007.

[234] "Commentary: Will the World Pattern Change?" *People's Daily*, April 4, 2003.

[235] "Who Won the Iraq War? China," *The Atlantic*, March 22, 2013; and "China and Iraq Announce Strategic Partnership," *The Diplomat*, December 23, 2015.

[236] "Most Indians Oppose War on Iraq, Survey," *Times of India*, February 4, 2003; "PM for Middle Path Approach to Iraq," *The Hindu*, March 11, 2003; "India's Devious Middle Path through the Iraq War," *Counterpunch*, April 15, 2003 and "Let India's Troops Go to Iraq," *The Wall Street Journal*, July 11, 2003.

The ground for military deals

As an extension of its expanding political and diplomatic connections to Asia, the Iraqi looking-East orientation gave a fresh start to Baghdad's defense and military relationship with Asian countries. The termination of a 14-year UN arms embargo against Iraq in 2004 enabled the legal purchasing of military equipment from the outside world. Moreover, the country's domestic chaos and its very fragile security situation compelled the new Iraqi leadership to immediately rebuild Iraq's rapidly draining military capabilities. Iraq's first choice was to tap into the high-tech arms industries of the West, but higher price tags as well as bureaucratic hurdles and the political strings attached frustrated the Iraqis.

Iraq in the post-Saddam era was to be ruled by a totally different political system, but the Middle East country could not quickly get rid of many restrictions and conditions which the West, the United States in particular, had imposed on Baghdad since the early 1990s. And despite its advantages as compared to the previous Ba'ath-dominated regime, the new political establishment did not manage to turn into a truly functioning democratic system, which left it virtually ineligible to receive certain military aid and arms from the West. Unrestrained by those pesky limitations and formidable obstacles, therefore, the quickly developing arms markets in the East were alluring to the Iraqis, though they were also able to acquire part of their military needs from Russia or less-known weapons producers outside the Eurasian region.

China was among the first Asian countries which pledged to strengthen its military and defense cooperation with post-war Iraq. By helping the Iraqis to build up their military capabilities, the Chinese were actually taking the opportunity to gain a fresh foothold in Iraq.[237] After all, China was not a newcomer to the Iraqi arms market. As a matter of fact, from 1982 to 1989 the Chinese had supplied close to $5 billion worth of weapons and military equipment to Iraq; a dazzling figure which accounted for around one-third of Beijing's total arms sales to the outside world in that period. Since the Chinese wished to position themselves as one of the top arms exporters in the world, the oil-rich country of Iraq with its huge military demand was too important to be lost to rivals.[238] Thus, after a hiatus of more than two and half decades, from 2007 onward China resumed its arms deals with Iraq,

---

[237] "China and Iraq Expand Energy and Defense Ties," *The Diplomat*, February 27, 2014; and "China, Iraq Ink Economic, Military Agreements during Abadi Visit," *The BRICS Post*, December 23, 2015.

[238] There has also been some reports about the rise of Chinese private security contractors in order to protect the East Asian power's elephantine assets abroad, especially in highly volatile and unstable countries like Iraq where China has massive investments. "Chinese Private Security Companies Go Global," *Financial Times*, February 26, 2017.

supplying it with various types of weapons and munitions including drones, air defense systems, and stealth fighters.[239]

Besides China, Iraq engaged in a major military contract with South Korea which in fact was "the most expensive defense export" in the history of the East Asian country. In December 2013, Iraq signed a deal with the defense contractor Korea Aerospace Industries (KAI) to purchase 24 light fighter jets. The total value of the deal was estimated to be around $2 billion; in addition to supplying 24 FA-50 aircraft, the agreement included training Iraqi pilots and other supportive measures for the air force for the ensuing two decades.[240] Iraq's needs were well aligned with Seoul's ambitious goal to become a major exporter of armaments and a top contender in the aviation industry in the world by 2020.[241] Like China, South Korea had also had some prior military deals with the Iraqis, harkening back to the Iran–Iraq War when they supplied weapons, employing both overt and covert methods, to the two warring parties.[242] Even during the international arms embargo against the Saddam regime, South Korea was still willing to negotiate other types of military deals with Iraq. As a case in point, the Iraqi government imported thousands of supply and transport vehicles for its elite Republican Guard between 2000 and 2002, and South Korea turned out to be one of the primary providers of those vehicles.[243]

Oil for the Orient: The raison d'être of a restructured state

Long before the onset of the Iraq War in 2003, the "oil factor" became a recurrent theme in discussions regarding the impending crisis in the Middle East. Many specialists as well as lay people believed firmly that the United States and its close partners were planning to invade Iraq, mainly for the sake of expropriating the country's massive oil wealth, under the guise of toppling the Saddam regime and eliminating the imminent threat of its supposed WMDs. This line of reasoning was never abandoned even after the American

---

[239] "Iraqis to Pay China $100 Million for Weapons for Police," *The Washington Post*, October 4, 2007; "China Joins Race to Arm Iraq," *Asharq Al-Awsat*, February 24, 2014; "China Helps Iraq Military Enter Drone Era," *BBC*, October 12, 2015; and "Use by Iraqi Military May Be a Boon for China-Made Drones," *The New York Times*, December 17, 2015.

[240] "S.Korea's KAI Sells Fighter Jets Worth $1.1 Billion to Iraq," *Reuters*, December 12, 2013; "Iraq to Receive 24 Fighter Jets from South Korea in 2017," *The Baghdad Post*, December 26, 2016; and "Iraq Receives 3rd Batch of South Korea's T-50 Fighters," *The Baghdad Post*, October 28, 2018.

[241] "After Iraq Acquires Fighter Jets, Envoy Praises Korean Alliance," *Korea Joongang Daily*, February 3, 2014.

[242] Shirzad Azad, *Koreans in Iran: Missiles, Markets and Myths* (New York: Algora Publishing, 2018), pp. 19–21.

[243] John F. Murphy, *The Evolving Dimensions of International Law: Hard Choices for the World Community* (New York: Cambridge University Press, 2010), p. 131.

coalition occupied Iraq and breathed new life into the country's economic system after rearranging its political system. The sputtering oil industry was a critical development which gave additional weight to the "oil factor" logic.[244] Many skeptics particularly focused on the oil industry, suggesting that Washington had overthrown the Ba'ath Party in Iraq to replace it with a new power structure congenial to the international oil business.[245]

For close to a decade and half, Iraq had been walled off from the world markets of energy by a harsh regime of international sanctions. The overthrow of Saddam and the removal of those sweeping sanctions, therefore, should have smoothed the way for integrating Iraq into the club of top crude exporters. As the world's fourth-largest holder of oil reserves, Iraq was to play a far bigger role in the international oil industry and become a major petroleum producer. This would have effectively reestablished the long pattern of rentier state in Iraq.[246] For that to happen, the new Iraq would need a massive injection of cold, hard cash and technology to revitalize its dilapidated and damaged oil industry. But Iraq was quite bankrupt, and many investors in the West were unwilling to risk their capital to get the Iraqi oil industry off the ground, due to its uncertainty and anarchic circumstances.

Meanwhile, amid all indiscriminate speculations and erratic developments involving the fate of Iraqi oil, the East turned out to be both an ace in the hole and joker in the pack. Asian countries gradually became the greatest investors in and largest consumers of Iraq's oil, encouraging the new Iraqi leadership to strengthen their diplomacy in the East. After positioning itself as the second biggest exporter of crude oil among the OPEC countries behind Saudi Arabia, Iraq prepared to supply some 67 percent of its entire petroleum exports to Asia alone by 2019. Like their seasoned counterparts in some other Middle Eastern countries, therefore, the neophyte authorities of Iraq soon realized that the East had become a pivotal player.[247] Once

---

[244] "Did the U.S. Invade Iraq to Contain China?" *Forbes*, January 7, 2011; "Iraq Invasion was about Oil," *The Guardian*, March 20, 2014; and "The Wars that really are about the Oil," *The Spectator*, August 30, 2014.

[245] Morton Winston, "The Humanitarian Argument for the Iraq War," *Journal of Human Rights*, Vol. 4, No. 1 (2005), pp. 45–51; Lawrence Freedman, "Iraq, Liberal Wars and Illiberal Containment," *Survival*, Vol. 48, No. 4 (2006), pp. 51–66; and Peter Stone, "The Rape of Mesopotamia: Behind the Looting of the Iraq Museum," *Public Archaeology*, Vol. 8, No. 4 (2009), pp. 378–381.

[246] Philippe Le Billon, "Corruption, Reconstruction and Oil Governance in Iraq," *Third World Quarterly*, Vol. 26, No. 4–5 (2005), pp. 685–703; and "3 Koreans Convicted of Bribery in Iraq," *Kurdish Globe*, May 5, 2009.

[247] "China Looks to Iraq to Secure Oil Supply," *Nikkei Asian Review*, June 15, 2018; "Iraq to Boost China Oil Sales by 60% as OPEC Giant Eyes Asia," *Bloomberg*, November 6, 2018; and "Iraq Approves China Drilling Deal for West Qurna Two Oilfield: Sources," *Reuters*, November 27, 2018.

the Iraqis found that they could establish a win–win partnership with these thirsty Eastern powers, they became more willing to turn their ongoing profit-sharing deals into real joint ventures with Asian countries.[248] This inclination and some other practical measures like building oil storage facilities in Asian countries could help Baghdad to potentially maintain its crude sales to the East over the long haul.[249]

Of course, no country in the East proved to be more critical to the Iraqi oil than China, whose growing footprint in the Middle Eastern country carried so much clout that it was dubbed the "real winner" of the Iraq War. To many people, it seemed that (thanks to the West) Iraq had emerged as a top oil producer and China had become its largest beneficiary. Even the American President, Barack Obama, accused the Chinese of "free riding" in Iraq, insinuating that the United States had done all the heavy lifting and China was now reaping the rewards.[250]

In reality, however, the new Iraq also became a major crude supplier to other oil-hungry Asian countries, including India, South Korea, and Japan.[251] Not only were China's overall investments in the post-Saddam Iraq far larger than those of all other Eastern nations, the Chinese were more willing and better equipped to assist the Iraqis with some of their political, economic and technological difficulties. The only problem was that Beijing would risk being accused of interfering in Iraq's domestic affairs, if the Chinese wanted to do the job their own way without collaborating with other key stakeholders in Iraq.[252]

One other important point is that China's attention to the oil-rich Iraq predated the Iraq War of 2003. China has been a net oil importer from 1993 onward, and its ferocious scramble for foreign energy resources pushed it

---

[248] The supply of crude oil ultimately rendered its impact, placing the Asian countries of China, India, and South Korea as the top three export partners of Iraq, respectively, whereas the architect of the Iraq War, the United States, was relegated to the fourth position.

[249] "Iraq Crisis to Dampen S. Korea's Growth: Report," *Korea Herald*, August 10, 2014; "Iraq's SOMO Chief Says Targeting More Crude Sells to Asian Markets," *Reuters*, March 18, 2018; and "Iraq May Build Oil Storage in Japan, South Korea to Drive Asian Sales," *Reuters*, March 27, 2018.

[250] "China Willing to Join Exxon at Giant Iraq Oil Field," *The Globe and Mail*, March 5, 2013; "China Is Reaping Biggest Benefits of Iraq Oil Boom," *The New York Times*, June 3, 2013, P. A1; and "If Anyone Bombs Iraq, Shouldn't it be China?" *Forbes*, June 15, 2014.

[251] "Korea's Costly Blunder in Iraq," *The Chosun Ilbo*, September 19, 2011; "South Korean Refiners to Drive up Term Crude Buying from Iraq," *Reuters*, February 28, 2014; and "Iraq Replaces Saudi Arabia as India's Lead Oil Supplier," *The Economic Times*, December 18, 2017.

[252] "Media Urge China to "Not Interfere' in Iraq," *BBC*, June 20, 2014; "Why China Stays Quiet on Iraq, Despite Being No. 1 Oil Investor," *Christian Science Monitor*, June 27, 2014; and "Xi Jinping Calls for Unity in Iraq, Confers with Ban Ki-moon on Middle East, Ebola, Ukraine," *South China Morning Post*, August 17, 2014.

naturally into the embrace of Middle East countries and other major oil-producing regions. At a time when a strict regime of international sanctions had been levied against the Saddam regime, the Chinese were not hesitant to pursue their oil interests in Baghdad. For instance, China became the third-biggest beneficiary of oil vouchers, a system which was allowed for Iraq under the UN oil-for-food program in the period from 1996 to 2003.

Like the French and Russians, the Chinese benefited from the Saddam regime's oil sales in exchange for offering weapons and other services required by Baghdad.[253] Another daring Chinese move was to sign a deal in 1997 with Saddam's Iraq to develop the Ahdab oil field in Wasit province, south of the capital. But the sanctions regimes forced the Chinese to postpone the profit-sharing oil deal until the downfall of the Ba'ath Party. The new political establishment in Baghdad revived that contract as early as 2007.[254]

The upshot of all those calculated measures was that Iraq gave its first major commercial oil contract to China in 2008.[255] And while Iraq's oil exports to China were nil in 2007, the Middle Eastern country managed to supply roughly nine percent of the total crude imported by the Chinese in less than a decade, overtaking Angola and Russia to become the second largest supplier of petroleum to China, right behind Saudi Arabia.[256]

Of course, this important development took place after the Chinese tactically reduced their crude purchases from some other major petroleum producers such as Saudi Arabia and especially Iran, whose share of international oil markets had been curtailed by sanctions.[257] China's state-owned corporations had been offered huge oil projects across Iraq, giving them the mandate to play a decisive role in modernizing and developing the shabby structures of the Iraqi oil industry. On top of that, the increasing presence of China in Iraqi's oil business only lent more weight to its role in other parts of Iraqi macro and micro economics, as was the case with some other Asian countries.[258]

---

[253] "Saddam Bribed China with Oil Deals, CIA Finds," *The Washington Times*, October 11, 2004.

[254] "Iraq Revives Saddam Deal with China," *Financial Times*, June 23, 2007.

[255] "Iraq and China Sign $3 Billion Oil Contract," *The Washington Post*, August 29, 2008.

[256] "Turmoil in Iraq 'Certain to Affect China Oil Prices'," *China Daily*, June 17, 2014; and "Iraq Takes Second Spot Among China Oil Sellers as Russia Cedes," *Bloomberg*, February 27, 2015.

[257] "China Keeps a Close Eye on Oil Interests in Iraq," *The New York Times*, June 17, 2014; and "Saudi Arabia's Oil Exports Fell in 2014 in 'Tough Year'," *Bloomberg*, February 18, 2015.

[258] "China Pushes for Bigger Role in Iraqi Reconstruction," *Arab News*, March 2, 2018.

Gearing toward non-oil business tie-in

Post-war Iraq's interactions with the East were not limited to a petro-leum partnership. As the Iraqi GDP gradually grew to $200 billion, including more than $60 billion in exports and $50 million in imports, its international economy deserved more recognition and attention. Exporting crude oil made up a lion's share of the Iraqi external trade, however, the bulk of the revenues had to be brought back in the form of imported goods and services. For many Asian countries, moreover, engaging in non-oil business with Iraq was a very effective strategy in order to gain a head start in signing lucrative contracts in the country's oil industry in addition to building better relationship with Baghdad in some other political, military, and cultural fields.[259] Once the post-conflict Iraq regained a semblance of stability, and security gradually improved in its restive provinces, the significance of building a "perfect part-nership" was accentuated by the new Iraqi rulers and their counterparts in the East. Both sides vowed to develop "all-out ties" and "comprehensive cooperation," signing a raft of non-oil business deals one year after another.[260]

High-level Iraqi delegations frequented the Asian capitals, seeking closer relations.[261] From pleading for the Chinese to write off the Saddam-era debts to visiting the headquarters of many Japanese and Korean companies, the new archons of Iraq had really little option but to tap into the resourceful East to rebuild their country.[262] While negotiating with their Iraqi counter-parts, Asian officials also called for their own hard-charging corporations and entrepreneurs to invest in different sectors of Iraq, ranging from trans-portation to telecommunications and from medical tourism to the entertain-ment industry.[263] This issue became even more critical for some major Asian economies when they faced growing trade deficits caused by importing larger cargos of Iraqi crude oil. As the East strived to reclaim its markets lost in Iraq due to sanctions and the post-war instability, a slew of Asian brands

---

[259] "S. Korea Secures 1st Oilfield in Iraq," *Korea Times*, November 11, 2007; "Taiwan Eases Visa Regulations for Iran, Iraq Businessmen," *BBC Monitoring Asia Pacific*, July 19, 2009; and "Taiwan to Donate Temporary Housing to Refugees in Iraq," *Taipei Times*, December 10, 2014, p. 3.

[260] Robert E. Looney, "The IMF's Return to Iraq," *Challenge*, Vol. 49, No. 3 (2006), pp. 26–47.

[261] "Iraq Seeks Stronger Korea Ties," *Korea Herald*, January 26, 2014; "Take Part in Reconstruction Work, Iraq Tells India," *The Hindu Business Line*, November 15, 2017; and "Iraqi PM Floats Joint Investment Fund for Projects with Japan," *Rudaw*, December 17, 2018.

[262] In 2010, China eventually concurred to cancel 80% of Iraq's $8.5 billion debt in line with the Paris Club agreements in November 2004 to write off that portion of the Saddam-era debt. "China Cancels 80% of Iraq's Debt," *Sydney Morning Herald*, February 3, 2010.

[263] "Shipbuilding Order for Two Harbor Work Ships Received from Iraq," *Toyota Tsusho Corporation*, May 11, 2018; and "Korean Lovers in Baghdad," *Al Jazeera*, November 15, 2018.

and trademarks soon accounted for the majority of goods imported by the populous Middle Eastern country.

In terms of overall bilateral trade, India and China made particularly strong progress in Iraq. By 2018, the two-way trade between the Iraqis and Indians had ratcheted up from a meager figure in the pre-conflict period to surprisingly $19 billion, making of Iraq the 10th largest trade partner for India.[264] China emerged eventually as the largest trading partner of Iraq, receiving a great deal of its exports. The record for Iraq's importation of Chinese goods was equally striking. China now supplies more than $8 billion or roughly 24 percent of Iraq's total imports. This is a telling figure if compared to 2003, when the total value of Chinese exports to Iraq was worth $56 million. In 2006, that depressing figure was still only around $490 million. The latest statistics, however, do not reveal the whole truth about the East's expanding trade with Iraq. The United Arab Emirates, for instance, emerged as a major trading partner of Iraq in the post-war period largely thanks to its entrepôt function and the re-exportation of Asian products into Iraqi markets.[265]

Construction: Bidding for a potentially new Middle East boom

The critical task of reconstructing Iraq was initially predicted to become "the largest nation-building project in history," overshadowing, in terms of complexity, cost, and size, even the reconstruction schemes implemented to rebuild Germany and Japan in the aftermath of World War II.[266] Before the scourge of the Islamic State (IS or ISIS) was given a chance to spread its terrorizing tentacles into large swathes of the Iraqi territory in 2014, the post-war political establishment was planning to invest, astonishingly, almost nine-hundred billion dollars on construction projects, including some $45 billion in Iraq's transportation infrastructures alone. By the time a majority of the IS militants were defeated in 2018, it was still projected that an austere reconstruction of Iraq would cost at least $88 billion.[267] In fact, there was more to such data than meets the eye. The country had been totally ravaged and reduced to rubble after more than three decades of large-

---

[264] "Indian Companies to Resume large-scale Exports to Iraq amid Global Blues," *Business Standard*, July 11, 2018; and "Are the Indian Companies Ready to Tap the Iraq Market? Huge Opportunities for Indian Companies in Iraq," *Financial Express*, December 12, 2018.

[265] "UAE–Iraq Trade Touches $7 Billion in 2016," *Iraqi Economists Network*, September 19, 2017; and "Widening the Gap," *Al-Ahram Weekly*, July 5, 2018.

[266] Peter V. Buren, *We Meant Well: How I Helped Lose the Battle for the Hearts and Minds of the Iraqi People* (New York: Metropolitan Books, 2011), p. 3.

[267] "Iraq Says Reconstruction after War on Islamic State to Cost $88 Billion," *Reuters*, February 12, 2018.

scale military conflict, sweeping international sanctions, foreign occupation, insurgency and civil war.[268]

Against the backdrop of that horrific history and initial upbeat expectations for assistance in rebuilding, however, the West simply walked away from its outstanding obligations regarding the post-Saddam Iraq. Many Western countries contributed very little, if any, to the international humanitarian programs launched to assist the reconstruction of Iraq.[269] In particular, the United States made it clear that the reconstruction of Iraq was not a priority for Washington, though American companies were going to be a major beneficiary of the business. As late as 2013, for instance, there happened to be at least 31 American companies in Iraq engaged in construction. Having set up the highest number of foreign construction companies in Iraq, then, the Americans were expected to form the financing backbone of the Iraqi reconstruction. But the hesitation of the government of the United States, as well as the large-scale chaos and instability that followed the rise of the IS, cast doubts upon the reliability of Western contractors, leaving the Iraqi leaders at the whim of Eastern nations such as China to rebuild their war-torn country.

In short, the Iraqi leaders needed the assistance of the Asians. In order to carry out and finance these reconstruction projects, they especially sought funds and technical know-how from a number of Asian countries with a long history of construction throughout the Middle East.[270] Since the first oil shock of 1973 some Asian nations, like Japan and particularly South Korea, had established an almost legendary record in the construction industry in the Middle East. Many of their contractors were now waiting in the wings to repeat their superlative performances and gain a foothold in the potentially huge market for reconstruction in Iraq. There was an Iraqi construction bonanza in the offing; every player from the cement industry to those erecting residential units could reap a windfall in Iraq.[271] Even many Indian contractors with a lean record in the construction business in the Middle

---

[268] "Unlike Iraq, Germany, Japan Knew Democracy," *Baltimore Sun*, March 30, 2003; "Iraqis Find Job Opportunities, New Lives in China," *NPR*, August 8, 2007; and Williamson Murray and Kevin M. Woods, *The Iran–Iraq War: A Military and Strategic History* (Cambridge, UK: Cambridge University Press, 2014), pp. 1–3.

[269] "Tokyo to Host Iraq Reconstruction Conference Oct. 13–14," *Kuwait News Agency*, September 6, 2004; and "Iraq's Allies Pledge $30 Billion toward Reconstruction," *The Wall Street Journal*, February 14, 2018.

[270] "On Visit, Iraq Asks China for Reconstruction Fund," *Fox News*, July 18, 2011; and "After 31 Years, Japan to Resume Loaning to Iraq," *Nikkei Asian Review*, March 30, 2017.

[271] "Iraq PM Asks China for Reconstruction Fund," *Asian Correspondent*, July 19, 2011; "S. Korea Firm to Sign $7.75 Billion Deal to Build Iraqi Homes," *Middle East Online*, May 24, 2012; and "China Keeps Eye on Oil Interests in Troubled Iraq," *The Economic Times*, June 19, 2014.

East were tempted to join the race.[272] But compared to the Indians, the Chinese and Koreans seemed to consider themselves more entitled to the imminent gold rush in Iraq.

Although China was most willing to pour its capital and technology into the oil industry, many other remunerative areas of construction and building also whetted the Chinese appetite for deeper engagement in the post-conflict Iraq. Not only were companies from China producing nearly 60 percent of the electricity in Baghdad, the Chinese had brought in some 15,000 workers to carry out other projects which were unrelated to oil or gas.[273] Given a high rate of unemployment among the Iraqi population, the importation of so many Chinese manual laborers did not go over very well. But for decades, many contractors from East Asia have adamantly insisted on bringing in their own workforce for foreign projects, primarily their own fellow citizens, in order to work more productively and inexpensively. It was, therefore, pretty much impossible to convince the risk-taking Chinese companies to undertake sophisticated and costly projects in Iraq while depending on local laborers.

More importantly, from 2013 onward the Chinese government strived to tie in the reconstruction business of Iraq with its mega project of "One Belt, One Road" (OBOR) or "Belt and Road Initiative" (BRI) in the Middle East.[274] Ruined by decades of shooting wars and heavy-handed sanctions, the Middle East country could be potentially the biggest ever jackpot of the international construction industry in the region. Iraq was an integral part of the historical route which the Chinese under Xi Jinping were now striving to revive, while a great deal of China's OBOR schemes had to do with construction and building. By dint of its critical location and huge resources, therefore, Iraq was certainly too important to be left out from the Chinese "Belt and Road" initiatives. That is why many Chinese officials often called for a speedy reconstruction process in Iraq, highlighting the Middle Eastern country's previously historical role as an important spot on the old Silk Road.[275]

---

[272] "India Offers Support for Reconstruction of Iraq," *The Hindu*, February 14, 2018.

[273] "China Prepares for Possible Iraq Evacuation," *Businessweek*, June 20, 2014; and "Stranded Chinese Workers Evacuated in Iraq," *Global Times*, June 27, 2014.

[274] "China to Actively Participate in Reconstruction of Iraq: Ambassador," *Xinhua*, February 15, 2018; "Opinion: China is Playing a Big Role in Iraqi Reconstruction," *CGTN*, February 17, 2018; "China Pushes for Bigger Role in Iraqi Reconstruction," *Arab News*, March 2, 2018; and "Chinese Envoy Calls for Accelerated Iraq Reconstruction," *China Daily*, November 14, 2018.

[275] "China Vows Active Role in Iraqi Post-war Reconstruction," *People's Daily*, April 25, 2017; "China Offers 80 m Yuans for Iraq Reconstruction," *The Baghdad Post*, July 12, 2017; and "Spotlight: Iraq, China Celebrate Silk Road Initiative on 60th Anniversary of Bilateral Ties," *Xinhua*, December 14, 2018.

The Koreans regarded their own contractors even more qualified and eligible than the Chinese to execute Iraq's construction projects. Some top Korean companies like Hyundai, Daewoo, Ssangyong, and Samsung had long been planning to expand their presence in Iraq. Hyundai, for instance, was impatient to retrieve more than $1.27 billion in overdue bills, including accrued interest, from the Saddam era. Long before Saddam invaded the neighboring Kuwait and triggered the Gulf crisis of 1990–1991, Korean companies like Hyundai had set their sights on Iraq.[276] But the ensuing international financial restrictions and sanctions severely limited the construction projects carried out by Korean companies in Iraq. Yet once South Korea sided closely with the United States over the course of the Iraq War in 2003, Korean companies found yet another reason to claim righteously why they were more suited than their Eastern rivals to carry through Iraqi reconstruction projects.[277]

Kurdistan: An encapsulation of looking East

Perhaps no part of the post-Saddam Iraq demonstrated more genuine interest in pursuing an inclusive orientation toward the East than the autonomous region of Kurdistan. Not only did the Kurdish region unexpectedly turn out to be safer and less volatile, it also experienced higher rates of economic progress and social development when juxtaposed with other parts of a crumbling Iraq. The highly ambitious and unified authorities of the Kurdistan Regional Government (KRG) soon launched their reconstruction and development programs, intending to break away totally from the central government in Baghdad after achieving a certain degree of political sophistication, military strength, and economic success.[278] The aspiring Kurds craved their own separate state independent of Iraq, and such a formidable task required them to do their own heavy lifting both internally and externally. As a corollary to that, the KRG officials paid particular attention to the East long before the last remaining relic of the Ba'ath Party was eradicated from Iraq.[279]

---

[276] "Korean Companies Busy in Iraq," *Korea Joongang Daily*, November 10, 1999.

[277] "Korean Companies Spot New Opportunities as Iraq Rebuilds," *Arirang*, March 20, 2013; "Companies Cast a Wary Eye on Iraq," *Korea Joongang Daily*, June 16, 2014; and "Iraqi President, South Korean Ambassador Discuss Reconstruction Plan," *Iraqi News*, November 4, 2018.

[278] Michael M. Gunter, *The Kurds: A Modern History* (Princeton, NJ: Markus Wiener Publishers, 2016), p. 101.

[279] Martin van Bruinessen, *Agha, Shaikh and State: The Social and Political Structures of Kurdistan* (London: Zed Books, 1992), pp. 14–15; and David McDowall, *A Modern History of the Kurds*, third edition (London and New York: I.B. Tauris, 2004), pp. 133–135.

Among the Asian countries, the KRG was willing to do more business with South Korea, Japan, and China. The Kurds had already hosted for a couple of years South Korea's army medics and engineers during the course of the Iraq War, fostering effective and durable connections to the Koreans.[280] Kurdistan, moreover, wished to learn from East Asia's development and industrialization experiences, benefiting from those Eastern countries' capital and technological investments in the Kurdish region.[281] The KRG offered more favorable terms for investments and technical assistance both in oil and non-energy sectors throughout the Kurdish region.[282] Sufficient capital and technological investments in the oil sector were of paramount importance as the KRG tried hard to ramp up its oil production to around one million barrels per day by 2020. The landlocked Kurds also hoped to be able to rely on Eastern countries as critical customers of their crude exports in the long run, though Asia was now importing part of the KRG's oil supplied through the Turkish port of Ceyhan.[283]

The promising situation of Kurdistan, however, triggered a rivalry of sorts among some Asian countries. Some in India criticized their own government for losing the game to China in Kurdistan, whereas the Chinese seemed to have engaged in one-upmanship with their Japanese and Korean counterparts there.[284] Like South Korea and Japan, China also set up a consulate in the political capital of Kurdistan, Erbil, turning the low-profile diplomatic mission into an important outpost for managing its growing interests in the Kurdish region. Moreover, some of the financial and technical assistance which Asian countries provided to the Iraqi government were going to end up somewhere in the Kurdish region.[285] In a good number of cases, Asian institutions were themselves involved directly in carrying out economic, social, and environmental projects financed by their affiliated governments. Two prominent Asian bodies which engaged in such activities in the Kurdish

[280] "Despite Protests, Seoul to Send Troops to Iraq for Reconstruction," *The New York Times*, April 2, 2003.

[281] "Iraqi Kurds Hope to Do Business with Japan, China, South Korea," *Sputnik*, June 4, 2016; and "PM Barzani Encourages Chinese Firms to Invest in Kurdistan," *Rudaw*, March 16, 2018.

[282] "Iraq Kurds in South Korean Oil Deal," *Kurdish Globe*, February 17, 2008; "Korea–Iraq Summit Due Next Week in Seoul," *Korea Times*, February 17, 2009; "Incheon to Support Iraq's Erbil Airport," *Kurdish Globe*, February 25, 2009; and "Hyundai Trucks Made in Iran for Iraqi Kurdistan," *Financial Tribune*, August 29, 2017.

[283] "KRG Prime Minister Says New South Korean Energy Deal Constitutional," *Kurdistan Regional Government*, February 15, 2008; and "Iraqi Kurdistan Oil May be Headed to China," *China Economic Review*, September 18, 2014.

[284] "India Lags behind China in Kurdistan Policy," *Hindustan Times*, September 20, 2014.

[285] "Japan's New Grant Assistance to Iraq," *Embassy of Japan in Iraq*, February 4, 2018; "KRG PM Barzani Thanks Japan for Helping to Solve Electricity Shortages," *Rudaw*, July 18, 2018; and "Korea Donates Aid to Yezidi Camp in Duhok," *Rudaw*, November 15, 2018.

region were the Japan International Cooperation Agency (JICA) and the Korean International Cooperation Agency (KOICA).[286]

On top of that, Asian countries were after some other strategic objectives through their collaboration with the KRG. The Kurds for now were a vital force helping the central government of Iraq to stabilize the country, and their role became even more critical after the rise of the IS in 2014.[287] For an Asian country like China with an expanding vested interest in the tumultuous Middle Eastern country, the partnership and cooperation of the Kurds was vital for Iraq's overall security and stability.[288] And if the Kurds succeeded to eventually establish their own sovereign state, the Eastern stakeholders could still have a better say in an independent Kurdistan because of their present crucial investments in the region administered by the KRG.[289] An independent Kurdish state would even be potentially advantageous to China, because the Chinese could use the Kurds as leverage to pressure Turkey not to further interfere with the Turkic-speaking Uighur minority of China, though the Chinese government has so far steadfastly endorsed the preservation of Iraqi territorial integrity with the KRG as an integral part of a unified Iraq.[290]

Conclusion

As the dust of the Iraqi invasion of 2003 began to settle, the country was transformed into a dreadful purgatory for about one and half decades to come. Sometimes it was even hard to realize who was really in charge in the post-war Iraq, since the commanding heights of the state had been handed over to some kind of shotgun coalition involving conservative nationalists, religious fundamentalists, and ethnic separatists. Many formative members

---

[286] "Signing of Japanese ODA Loan Agreements with Iraq: Contributing to Reconstruction through the Provision and Repair of Water and Irrigation Facilities," *Japan International Cooperation Agency*, May 7, 2018.

[287] Richard Andres, "The Afghan Model in Northern Iraq," *Journal of Strategic Studies*, Vol. 29, No. 3 (2006), pp. 395–422; and "Iraq Leader in Japan for Talks with Abe on Peace, Reconstruction," *The Asahi Shimbun*, April 5, 2018.

[288] Bill Park, "The Kurds and Post-Saddam Political Arrangements in Iraq," *The Adelphi Papers*, Vol. 45, No. 374 (2005), pp. 29–48; and Michael M. Gunter, "Arab–Kurdish Relations and the Future of Iraq," *Third World Quarterly*, Vol. 32, No. 9 (2011), pp. 1623–1635.

[289] "Xinjiang Militants Being Trained in Syria and Iraq, Says Special Chinese Envoy," *South China Morning Post*," July 28, 2014; "The Secret Lives of Chinese Missionaries in Northern Iraq," *South China Morning Post*, July 16, 2017; and "Baghdad University Hosts the Chinese Ambassador," *University of Baghdad*, January 10, 2019.

[290] "China Supports Iraq to Maintain Sovereignty, Calls for Inclusive Gov't: Envoy," *People's Daily*, July 8, 2014; "Turkey's Ambiguous Policies Help Terrorists Join IS Jihadist Group: Analyst," *Global Times*, December 15, 2014; and "300 Chinese are Fighting alongside ISIS in Iraq, Syria," *New York Post*, December 15, 2014.

of each group still harbored serious grudges and grievances against their own colleagues, let alone other members of their coalition. But in spite of their irreconcilable differences and clashing views, they all wanted to remain part of the emerging governing class and thereby benefit from its advantages and perks. And while no single group among the ruling coalition could present a compelling blueprint for the peace and prosperity of Iraq in long run, almost all of them were unusually in favor of finding ways to patch up the political problems and get the economy moving again — at least for now.

After many years of conflicts and sanctions, however, post-war Iraq was a bleak and desolate landscape devoid of resources. The West showed no firm commitment to a thorough program of reconstruction and nation-building, after all the hopeful expectations it had created in the run-up to the invasion of 2003. Turning to the East, therefore, without acknowledging in every respect the previous connections between the two sides, the new Iraqi state managed to secure a great deal of ready funds and technological materials in order to start the work. Iraq embarked upon a looking-East orientation to draw rich Asian countries into close politico-economic and technological cooperation with Baghdad. The Iraqis focused on fast results to be achieved by investments from Asian countries, but they also knew full well that the future of their country hinged, to a great extent, on fostering long term multifaceted interactions with the East.

Many Asian nations were equally eager to renew their relationship with Iraq. Some of those countries had strived to maintain a semblance of bilateral connections to Baghdad even in the atmosphere of military conflicts or severe international restrictions. But the stakes were now much higher, as Iraq was going to be opened up to foreign investors and could potentially become a hive of reconstruction and other economic activities. Poverty and destitution oozed from every pore of the country, but it was an oil rich land and could, with time, regenerate its lost vitality. And despite all lurking dangers and hidden perils, Iraq was able to provide some safe and peaceful space for Asian investments. The reluctance of Western businesses to pour their capital and technical know-how into the new Iraq were not going to discourage Eastern investors, either; in fact, it gave them a free hand to pick up the parts most conducive to their own interests.

Chapter 5. Turkey: Commingling Ideational and Material Interests

Since the ascendancy of the Justice and Development Party (*Adalet ve Kalkınma Partisi*, or AKP) in 2002, Turkey has reappraised its foreign policy priorities in critical ways. Led by the current President, Recep Tayyip Erdoğan, the Turkish political establishment has been clear about resetting its foreign policy by distancing the country from the West in favor of building better connections to other regions. Turkey has certainly not abandoned its long-cherished aspiration of joining the European Union (EU), but the leadership of Turkey has demonstrated over the past years that the Turks are no longer willing to pay any demeaning price just to achieve that goal. Moreover, unprecedentedly, the Turkish leaders have sometimes even gone out of their way to criticize international political, economic and even cultural policies of major Western countries — no matter if they are still a committed and active member of the North Atlantic Treaty Organization (NATO).

As time goes by, Turkey's attitude toward the West has been more and more cool and aloof, while it warms up more and more to the East. The Eastward leanings of Turkey under the AKP are, however, to be understood to mean cultivating friendly relations with most Middle Eastern countries except, of course, the Jewish state of Israel.

This keen desire to reorient Ankara's relations with countries across the Middle East is demonstrated by regular high-level political visits and increasing volumes of economic exchanges. Many observers have had to adjust their own understanding of Turkish foreign policy priorities based on Ankara's new behavior, as their approach to the Mideast region seems to serve as a thermometer by which one might gauge the commensurate cooling off towards the Western nations.[291]

And it turns out that the wider Middle East is only one part of Turkey's new inclination toward the East. Like so many others, Turkey is also cozying up to the rising powers of Asia. That is in some ways complementary to Ankara's new policy toward the Middle East in general, but it is far from being a mere extension of it. Yet while scholars and journalists have shone a spotlight on Turkey's relationship with the Middle East since the early 2000s, research on Turkey's recent approach to Asia has, for the most part, remained sparse and scattered.

There have certainly been plenty of ups and downs in Ankara's inter-actions with Asian countries, but many crucial developments have been obscured by Turkey's hectic relations with other parts of the world, the Middle East in particular. Bearing that in mind, what are the defining char-acteristics of Turkey's looking-East policy under the AKP? Why did the Turkish state need to formulate its own looking-East approach in the first place? How has Turkey's new orientation played out in practice? Which areas of bilateral interactions were most promising? How about Turkey's counterparts farther East? Have Asian countries generally been willing to reciprocate?

A beneficial balance: Reverting to roots and seeking rewards

As a country with territory in both Europe and Asia, the modern Turkish Republic, heir to the Ottoman Empire, is a proud political entity long asso-ciated with a dual identity. Throughout the twentieth century, the Turks strived from one decade to the next to emphasize their European identity without in any way diminishing their Asian credentials. Decades of rule by worldly and secular elements played a critical role in directing the country toward Europe and implanting a pro-Western propensity and forward-looking life-style in the minds of many Turkish citizens.[292] Still, the religious traditionalists and Islamist forces of Turkey did not disappear in total, either in politico-economic or in socio-cultural terms.[293] They occasionally shook the secular establishment, but each time they were stopped from bringing

---

[291] Aaron Stein, *Turkey's New Foreign Policy: Davutoglu, the AKP and the Pursuit of Regional Order* (London: Royal United Services Institute for Defence and Security Studies, 2014), p. 59.

[292] "Turkey is a European Country," *Daily Sabah*, September 6, 2018; and "Trump Warned Turkey Punishment Could 'Hand Middle East to China'," *Express*, August 21, 2019.

[293] Henri J. Barkey, "Turkey and the New Middle East: A Geopolitical Exploration," in Henri J. Barkey, ed., *Reluctant Neighbor: Turkey's Role in the Middle East* (Washington D.C.: The United States Institute of Peace Press, 1996), pp. 25–43.

down the system as it was safeguarded by the army, the ultimate custodian of Turkish secularism. It was only in 2002 that the AKP-led Islamists managed to unseat the secularist politicians, and they have remained at the helm of state affairs for the longest period in contemporary Turkish history.[294]

However, by the time Erdoğan's cunning dog-whistle politics and his bewildering blend of "Islamism and populism" became the order of the day, secularism and Western-leaning attitudes were so deeply embedded in the society that they could not be disregarded entirely. At the least, the AKP apparatchiks favored a balance between the West and the East. The party obviously had no intention of continuing to seek closer ties with Western countries as many among secular forces expected,[295] but even Erdoğan's emotional attachment to the East was not tinged with a blunt anti-Westernism (a trend seen among some of his obstreperous counterparts in the Middle East, where the Turkish leader had now been dubbed by some as the new "caliph of the Muslims"). The AKP leadership certainly felt more affinity with the Middle East, but it did not dare to abandon the long-term quest to be a full member of the European club. Erdoğan and his clique only needed to convince the public why their country needed to tilt more toward the East — without burning bridges with the West.[296]

Considering the Muslim countries in the immediate neighborhood, the Erdoğan-led AKP asserted that Turkey had long enjoyed geopolitical as well as socio-cultural connections to countries in the Middle East, the Caucasus and Central Asia.[297] Instead of adhering to realpolitik in wheeling and dealing with these countries, the sanguine Turkish leaders now aimed to pursue a foreign policy of "zero problems" as the best approach to win over their fellow Muslim neighbors.[298] Beyond reinforcing this identity, moreover,

---

[294] Graham E. Fuller, *The New Turkish Republic: Turkey as a Pivotal State in the Muslim World* (Washington, D.C.: United States Institute of Peace Press, 2007).

[295] Some in the West were quietly happy to see Turkey's further tilt toward the Middle East, and generally the East. By enumerating some dismal records of encroachment upon civil liberties and human rights violations, on a par with China in terms of the number of political dissenters and journalists jailed, those Westerners were actually questioning Turkey's eligibility to be admitted into the EU and other high profile institutions in the West. Other critics in the West considered the deafening silence and double-standard behaviors of their own governments with regard to the human rights dossier of allies like Turkey and Israel as a sure-fire way to further tarnish Western democratic principles and values among the international community. For instance, see: Chris Morris, *The New Turkey: The Quiet Revolution on the Edge of Europe* (London: Granta Publications, 2005), p. 6; and Stephen M. Walt, *The Hell of Good Intentions: America's Foreign Policy Elite and the Decline of U.S. Primacy* (New York: Farrar, Straus and Giroux, 2018), pp. 43, 68.

[296] Bill Park, "Populism and Islamism in Turkey," *Turkish Studies*, Vol. 19, No. 2 (November 2017), pp. 169–175.

[297] Stein, p. 28.

[298] Ahmet Davutoğlu, "Zero Problems in a New Era: Realpolitik is No Answer to the Challenges Posed by the Arab Spring," *Foreign Policy*, March 21, 2013.

Turkey aimed to take the lead in terms of shaping a new regional order, one capable of meeting the challenges of a newly globalizing region. By focusing on shared elements of identity and destiny, the Turks sought to show themselves to be entitled to benefit from the economic rewards the Muslim world could offer. Much like the AKP's strategy to maintain an equilibrium between the Western and Eastern loyalties of Turkey, therefore, its looking-East orientation aimed to juxtapose the Turkish politico-cultural identity with its economic and technological interests.[299]

With respect to Asia, the Turks had good reason for looking East. The AKP leaders understood that a rising Asia would likely become a pillar in the emerging new international order and thus could offer some balance as the West-led order inexorably tottered. The growing power and influence of Eastern countries would potentially provide the Turks with many new opportunities. After all, Turkey had previously been involved in Asia, sometimes very deeply, and its partial Asian identity would serve as an asset. Forging closer connections to rising Asian countries could also damp down some severe domestic criticism in the light of the AKP's growing distance from the West and its increasing involvement in Middle Eastern affairs. The AKP could at least convince many of its critics that improving ties with Asian countries would provide economic and technologic advantages.[300]

One other important rationale behind Turkey's determination to look-East was, however, their growing alarm at the surging flow of Asian brands and products, impinging on Turkish economic prospects at home and abroad. For decades, Turkey had been producing a variety of relatively cheap and appealing products for domestic consumption and for export to neighboring countries. But profitable Turkish markets were now losing their competitive advantage to Asian goods. Turkey's primarily labor-intensive products and the country's technological shortcomings now made it very susceptible to the flow of affordable and alluring modern products supplied by Asian countries.[301] The looking-East orientation was certainly not going to reverse this disquieting trend, but it could help Turkey to make up for some part of its inevitable losses. The Turks could at least look for some sort of symbiotic relationship with their Asian counterparts in areas favorable to them.

---

[299] Charles A. Kupchan, *How Enemies Become Friends: The Sources of Stable Peace* (Princeton, NJ: Princeton University Press, 2010), p. 414.
[300] Bill Park, *Modern Turkey: People, State and Foreign Policy in a Globalized World* (Abingdon and New York: Routledge, 2012), p. 110.
[301] Park, p. 69.

Subscribing to multipolarity: Politico-strategic motives

Under the AKP, Turkey's pro-Eastern policy was more than a business-like bid to diversify its allies and partners. Turkey continued to edge away from some pivotal countries in the West, to the great surprise of many, adding vigor to the looking-East approach, but fundamentally the Turkish move was ultimately an acknowledgement of the emerging multipolar order. Since the Turks seemed to be less than delighted with the way the West was treating them, they would not mind terribly much if the US-led domineering world order were replaced by a new multipolar system, and they were not reluctant to contribute to such an eventuality.[302] The emergent Asian powers were certainly among the major contenders to shape the modality and function of such a new arrangement. This time, however, the Turkish leaders wanted to avoid being reliant on just one partner, and they did all they could to build links with most of the nations in the East.[303]

Turkey managed to strengthen its connections to every country in Northeast Asia, including Taiwan and North Korea.[304] The Turks had long kept up informal diplomatic and commercial interactions with the Taiwanese, while Ankara's normalization of its diplomatic relationship with Pyongyang in the early 2000s quietly started to move through the gears under the AKP leadership. By comparison, three other, bigger players in the region were front and center in Turkey's looking-East plans. Turkey's developing ties with the Republic of Korea were elevated to the level of "strategic partnership" in 2012 as the Turks' "blood brothers" in South Korea were now delighted to make the most of Turkey's "pivot to Asia."[305] Similar to the ROK, the Turkish state had long been on good terms with Japan, and the growing multifaceted connections between the two countries needed to be accentuated in the face of the "China challenge." Because of their financial muscle and advanced technological know-how, moreover, the Japanese were perceived to be more

---

[302] Philip Robins, *Suits and Uniforms: Turkish Foreign Policy since the Cold War* (London: C. Hurst & Co., 2003), p. 208.

[303] "Taiwan's Overtures toward Turkey," *Cihan News Agency*, May 31, 2014; and "Why Turkey Matters to Asia," *The Straits Times*, August 25, 2017.

[304] "U.S. Imposes Sanctions on Turkish Company for Trade with North Korea," *The New York Times*, October 4, 2018.

[305] Turkey was a major foreign participant in the Korean War of 1950–1953, and more than two thousands of Turkish soldiers were either killed or seriously wounded over the course of the internecine conflict. "Turkey and South Korea: Blood Brothers for 60 Years," *Anadolu Agency*, November 17, 2015; "South Korea Praises Turkey's Help during Korean War," *Hurriyet Daily News*, July 27, 2018; and Shirzad Azad, *East Asian Politico-Economic Ties with the Middle East: Newcomers, Trailblazers, and Unsung Stakeholders* (New York: Algora Publishing, 2019), pp. 81, 107.

---

agreeable to Turkey's looking-East requirements than many other well-to-do Asian powers.[306]

Unlike South Korea, Japan and some other rising Asian countries, however, China represented in some regards a double-edged sword for Turkey. Since the end of the Cold War and the disintegration of the Soviet Union, the Turks had strived to promote their influence and interests throughout Central Asia and the Caucasus, capitalizing on the identity and historical legacy they shared with the peoples located there. Since Turkey's neo-Ottomanism under the AKP saw Central Asia as a core of its "strategic depth," the Turks found it increasingly difficult to tolerate the encroaching tide of Chinese presence in the region.[307] China's ever-expanding role in Central Asia could make it all but impossible to establish the new pan-Turkish empire Erdoğan envisioned, stretching as far east as China's Xinjiang Province, where the Turkic-speaking Uighur minority were starting to rely on the Turks as their only support against maltreatment at the hands of China. Turkey regards some of China's policies in Xinjiang as a "shame for humanity," while the Chinese accuse the Turks of suffering from their "pan-Turkism complex."[308] Intensified by geopolitical rivalries and other important issues, the Turkish–Chinese clash over the Uighurs seems unlikely to dissipate anytime soon.

Despite their conflicting objectives and grave disagreements over a wide range of issues, China had become a powerful player for Turkey to reckon with in international politics. In addition to its growing political and military clout, China's fast-growing economic and financial capabilities offered a well-timed substitute for Turkey's dwindling opportunities in the West.[309]

The Turkish aspirants were also counting on the Chinese to one day allow them to become a full member of international and regional institutions such as the BRICS and especially the Shanghai Cooperation Organization (SCO). By talking up the significance of deepening "strategic mutual trust" between Beijing and Ankara, the Chinese leaders were indeed prepared to lend a helping hand to their Turkish counterparts. The political and economic rivalry between the two countries might encompass large swathes of territory extending from Central Asia to Africa, but the Chinese were keen to keep the Turks satisfied, or at least silent, on the Uighur matter because the

---

[306] "Turkey, Japan to Cooperate on Tech," *Daily Sabah*, November 7, 2014.
[307] William M. Hale, *Turkish Foreign Policy, 1774–2000* (London: Frank Cass, 2000), p. 91.
[308] "Passports for Uyghurs' Story Shadows Turkey's Relations with PRC," *Asia Times*, July 13, 2015; "Turkey Calls China's Uighur Detentions 'Shame for Humanity'," *Nikkei Asian Review*, February 13, 2019; and "Turkey in no Position to Judge Xinjiang," *Global Times*, February 11, 2019.
[309] Hale, p. 333.

global media and press were set abuzz almost any time Turkey officially aired its displeasure about China's misconduct in Xinjiang.[310] Moreover, Turkey's increasing alienation from the West was seen to dovetail neatly with various Chinese policies and strategies.[311]

In South Asia, Turkey had a complicated relationship with India, just as it did with China. Part of the friction with India stemmed from Ankara's sympathy with Pakistan over the Kashmir issue. Compared to former secular governments in Turkey, the Islamist AKP was indubitably more inclined to side with the Kashmiri Muslims. But India was also a rising power with great promise. Thus, Turkey's current pattern of political alliances dictated it should be nice to India, even if good connections to China appeared to offer more economic rewards.[312] At present, India is perceived to be lesser challenge than China to Turkey's interests in Central Asia and the greater Middle East. All in all, by following a pragmatist approach vis-à-vis India, the looking-East drive could put to good use Turkey's popularity and soft power among some 400 million Muslims in South Asia in the long run.

Turkey was even more enthusiastic about fostering closer connections to member countries of the Association of Southeast Asian Nations (ASEAN). The Turks even flattered the ASEAN by expressing their inclination to join the homogeneous regional bloc.[313] From signing the Treaty of Amity and Cooperation with ASEAN in 2010 to attending the ASEAN summit of 2013, Ankara's move toward Southeast Asia exemplified the zeal and perseverance of its looking-East orientation. Viewing the region as a huge market of around 650 million people, larger than the EU market, once Ankara inaugurated its embassy in Laos in November 2018, it managed to open embassies in all ASEAN countries.[314]

Many ASEAN members were equally in favor of developing good relations with the Turks. Turkey's moderate Islam was seen as a positive role model for a large community of Muslims residing across the ASEAN region, while its strategic location could amply facilitate ASEAN's access to Europe and the Middle East.[315] Thus ASEAN gave the Turks observer status in 2014, before agreeing to accept Turkey as a sectoral dialogue partner in 2017 —

---

[310] "Turkey Jockeys with China for Influence in Africa," *Nikkei Asian Review*, May 12, 2018.
[311] Steven A. Cook, *False Dawn: Protest, Democracy, and Violence in the New Middle East* (New York: Oxford University Press, 2017), p. 165.
[312] Stephen Kinzer, *Reset: Iran, Turkey, and America's Future* (New York: Times Books, 2010), p. 11.
[313] "Turkey Wants to Become ASEAN Member," *Trend News Agency*, July 31, 2015.
[314] "Turkey Inaugurates Embassy in Laos," *Anadolu Agency*, November 7, 2018.
[315] "Malaysia Turkey's Gateway into Asean'," *The Borneo Post*, April 7, 2018; and "Iran FM to Visit Singapore to Join ASEAN Treaty," *Xinhua*, July 29, 2018.

though Ankara is still aspiring to a higher formal standing within the South-east Asian bloc.[316]

Pursuing unparalleled military and defense deals with Asia

One less-known aspect of the Turks' looking-East orientation is a major overhaul in the country's defense and military interactions with Asian nations. Although it is easy to understand Turkey's taking a new direction in foreign policy in the wake of the AKP's political triumph in the early 2000s, the Turks' desire for a greater military and defense engagement with Asia was more perplexing. As an important NATO member since 1952, Turkey used to be influenced heavily by the defense and security priorities prescribed by that exclusive organization. The NATO alliance also had an equally significant impact on Turkey's international interactions. Turkey's military deals and arms production were ineluctably prioritized on the basis of attachment to NATO,[317] but they received major amounts of military aid and training over the decades, provided by the more advanced and affluent NATO members, the United States in particular.

Now, however, the Turkish army has surprisingly played an active role in Ankara's new military and defense relationship with Asian countries. Such a critical development may seem counterintuitive, especially for those who would have expected a neat Manichaean dichotomy between the AKP-led Islamism and the army-led Kemalism. In fact, the Turkish army, as the guardian of the Republic, wielded enormous power and influence over Turkey's foreign and security policies. Regarded as a force for socio-political stability and modernization, the army's role extended far beyond conventional national defense and security matters. Given this background, it was reasonable that some Turkish observers inside and outside the country might identify a new dynamics of power politics in Turkey at the cost of the army.[318] This idea that the army suffered a declining, and even distorted, role under the Erdoğan-led rule after 2002 became more credible in the aftermath

---

[316] "Turkey's Rough Road in Engaging Asean," *Bangkok Post*, February 20, 2018; "PM Hails Trip to Turkey and Europe as 'a Great Success'," *The Phnom Penh Post*, October 26, 2018; and "Singapore Hosts First Turkey–ASEAN Trilateral Meeting," *Daily Sabah*, August 1, 2018.

[317] Stockholm International Peace Research, *SIPRI Yearbook 2011: Armaments, Disarmament and International Security* (New York: Oxford University Press, 2011), pp. 245–246.

[318] William Hale, *Turkish Politics and the Military* (London and New York: Routledge, 1994), p. vii; and Steven A. Cook, *Ruling But Not Governing: The Military and Political Development in Egypt, Algeria, and Turkey* (Baltimore, MD: The Johns Hopkins University Press, 2007), p. 103.

of the so-called botched coup in July 2016, when thousands of army officers and soldiers were arrested and prosecuted by the state apparatuses.[319]

Whether or not arguments about a newly dynamic civilian–military relationship in Turkey could withstand scrutiny, the country's growing military and defense connections to Asia under the looking-East approach have been unprecedented. Given the East's enormous potential to contribute to Turkey's new plans for diversification in the military and defense realms, the Turks have tried especially to curry favor with those Asian countries which could best meet those objectives.[320] They had long relied on the West for their arms imports, while countries in the Middle East, Central Asia and the Caucasus used to be the main customers of Turkey's own arms production. The Turks aimed to change this long-established pattern as much as possible by taking advantage of the many new opportunities Asian countries offered. They wanted both to identify new clients for their military exports and to gain more sophisticated and advanced armaments.[321]

With regard to arms exports, Turkey courted particularly ASEAN countries, though Pakistan in South Asia was another good target market as well.[322] In addition to proactive participation in ASEAN defense exhibitions, the Turks made a number of military deals with Malaysia, Indonesia, and the Philippines. ASEAN is in a position to help Turkey reach its ambitious goal of exporting some $25 billion worth of armaments by 2023.[323] Besides purchasing Turkish arms, some ASEAN countries are seen as potential partners in achieving their equally-important objective of self-sufficiency in the defense industry before the mid-2020s. A case in point is Indonesia, whose defense company PT Pindad entered into an agreement with Turkish armored vehicle manufacturer FNSS to jointly produce the KAPLAN medium-weight battle tanks since 2015. The Middle East, ASEAN, South and Central Asian nations have been earmarked as potential markets for the joint product of military tanks between Turkey and Indonesia.[324]

---

[319] Cook, p. 169.

[320] "Turkey Sixth Largest Arms Importer, Report Reveals," *Hurriyet Daily News*, February 22, 2016; and "Turkish FM Cements Security Ties with China," *Hurriyet Daily News*, August 7, 2017.

[321] "Turkey Steps up Arms Sales to South and Southeast Asia," *Nikkei Asian Review*, January 12, 2018.

[322] "Pakistan, Turkey Sign Deal for 30 Helicopter Gunships," *The Diplomat*, July 16, 2018.

[323] "Turkish Defense Industry Eyes ASEAN Aerospace Market," *Daily Sabah*, November 7, 2017; "Turkey Biggest Participant at Defense Exhibition in Southeast Asia," *Daily Sabah*, April 16, 2018; and "A New Philippines–Turkey Military Helicopter Deal?" *The Diplomat*, December 4, 2018.

[324] "Where Are Indonesia–Turkey Military Ties?" *The Diplomat*, September 12, 2017; "Pakistan to Receive 30 Helicopter Gunships from Turkey," *The Diplomat*, June 7, 2018; and "Kuwait Looks to Turkish and Chinese Military Power," *Arab News*, October 19, 2018.

Since 2004, therefore, Turkey under the AKP has made serious efforts to enhance its technical skills in developing and designing military products, encouraging technology transfer through bilateral arms production collaborations involving Asian countries. With the dual goals of self-sufficiency and boosting arms exports, the Turks spent roughly $1 billion in 2004 for purchasing and technology transfer of South Korean K9 howitzers, which Turkey later renamed Firtina, meaning "storm" in the Turkish language.[325] In 2007, moreover, Turkish Aerospace Industries (TAI) signed a $350 million contract with Korea Aerospace Industries (KAI) to buy at least 40 KT-1T basic trainer aircraft from South Korea. With an eye to replacing its aging US-made T-37 trainer planes with the KT-1Ts, Turkey considered the deal essential for expediting its national program of designing, developing, and producing an indigenous basic trainer aircraft named Hurkus. The Turks and their South Korean partners are also evaluating the feasibility of jointly developing a fighter aircraft after 2020.[326]

In its quest for greater defense and military cooperation with the East, however, Turkey went out of its way to antagonize its NATO allies. The most contentious case involved a deal worth $3.4 billion awarded to China to develop a long-range missile defense system for Turkey. The news soon caused a buzz in Western media and policy circles, as it was something of a shock for an important member of NATO to select the Chinese Precision Machinery Import and Export Corp as its preferred candidate. As widely expected, Ankara came under mounting pressures by major NATO members, especially the United States, to immediately scrap the deal. In addition to regarding the Turkish move as an indignity, NATO nations objected that their security could be jeopardized by letting the Turks deploy Chinese military equipment of subpar quality. It would also mean that Western arms producers would lose out on a lucrative contract, setting a disastrous precedent. As a consequence, the Turks eventually did an about-face, cancelled the deal with China and decided instead to develop the project themselves utilizing domestic resources.[327]

---

[325] "Korea Inks $400 Million Tank Deal with Turkey," July 30, 2008; and "Turkey Confirms Trainer Deal with South Korea," *Defense News*, April 12, 2015.

[326] "Turkey Hit Syria with S. Korean-designed Howitzers," *Hurriyet Daily News*, October 4, 2012; and "Korea to Deliver 48 K9 Self-propelled Howitzers to Finland," *Korea Herald*, February 21, 2017.

[327] "Turkey Confirms It Cancels Defence System Tender Awarded to China," *Reuters*, November 17, 2015.

Commercial connections: Seeking substitution and symmetry

Still, in order to reduce its reliance on the West and hedge against a gradual deterioration of its political and security relationship with major Western countries, no strategy was thought to offer more potential for Turkey than engaging in larger volume of economic and financial interactions with the East. For decades, the Turks had largely been at the whim of Western, especially European, markets to export their agricultural goods and textile products. But Turkish businesses were increasingly feeling the pinch as they encountered more and more obstacles to elevating their export figures to Western markets. But it wasn't the AKP's standoffish attitude that led to Turkey's dwindling economic opportunities in the West. Quite to the contrary, it was Turkey's shrinking access to Western markets that had made the Erdoğan-led AKP more confident in its increasing detachment from the West in favor of the East.[328]

Among Eastern countries, no nation appeared to be more promising than China, though the two countries were sometimes at loggerheads over political and security issues involving not only the Uighurs but parts of Central Asia and the Middle East as well (the Syrian civil war included).[329] The stakes became much higher when the Chinese announced their "One Belt, One Road" initiative to revive the ancient Silk Road, in which Turkey could obviously serve as a crucial link.[330] Since the end of the Cold War, the Turks had tried to gain a foothold throughout Central Asia, and the Chinese Belt and Road projects could provide them with a unique opportunity to further promote their vital interests in the region.[331] Moreover, the bilateral trade between the two countries skyrocketed over the years, jumping from some $1 billion in 2000 to around $19.5 billion in 2010, $26.3 billion in 2017, and $23.63 in 2018. Turkey and China even ditched the dollar in order to trade with each other using local currencies.[332] The Turks were, however, deeply uneasy about the constant, huge trade deficits (roughly $20.5 billion in 2017 and $18 billion in 2018 alone) in favor of China.[333] To partially rectify this

---

[328] "Chinese Envoy to Ankara: Middle Corridor Project will Bring China, Turkey Together in Line with Bilateral Strategies," *Daily Sabah*, November 13, 2017; and "Turkey Eyes Stronger Regional, Global Role with Closer China Ties," *Global Times*, June 15, 2018.

[329] "Xinjiang Terrorists Finding Training, Support in Syria, Turkey," *Global Times*, July 1, 2013; and "China Accuses Turkey of Aiding Uighurs," *Financial Times*, July 12, 2015.

[330] "Turkey Opens Rail Link for New Silk Road," *The Times*, October 31, 2017.

[331] "Why is Turkey so Eager to be led down the Belt and Road?" *East Asia Forum*, October 28, 2017.

[332] "Chinese Business Magnates Flock to Turkey," *Middle East Monitor*, August 17, 2018; and "Turkey to Trade in Local Currencies with Iran, China," *Press TV*, September 3, 2018.

[333] Data taken from Turkish Statistical Institute (commonly known as TurkStat) available at www.turkstat.gov.tr.

growing commercial imbalance, the Chinese were often encouraged at the highest level to ratchet up their share of direct international investments in Turkey.[334]

Meanwhile, Turkey was suffering from equally high trade deficits with other East Asian economies, including Japan and South Korea. In 2018, for instance, Turkey imported some $4 billion of Japanese goods but the total value of its exports to them was less than $700 million. The presence of more than 220 Japanese companies in Turkey has hardly made a dent in the edifice of these perpetual trade imbalances. To chip away at this problem, Japan and Turkey started since 2014 to negotiate a free trade agreement (FTA) to replace the existing pact of Reciprocal Promotion and Protection of Investments which they had signed in 1993.[335] Despite some serious disagreement over a Japanese proposal for abolishing Turkish tariffs on imported cars and auto parts, the two sides are still pushing for a final FTA to be hammered out in the near future.[336] Any breakthrough in their ongoing negotiations would help Japan to expand its international markets by taking advantage of Turkey as a manufacturing base for its companies operating so close to Europe, Africa, and the wider Middle East.[337]

With regard to South Korea, progress was made more quickly and FTA agreements have been signed covering numerous areas of commerce. In 2013, Turkey and the ROK's FTA on physical goods took effect, and the two countries managed in 2015 to sign another bilateral agreement covering the service and investment sectors. The latter FTA actually went into effect in only 2018, with the three-year standstill being mostly related to Turkey's own domestic conditions.

While the outcome of such bilateral accords and other economic negotiations may reduce the trade disparities between Ankara and Seoul a bit, Turkey has experienced significant trade deficits with South Korea for several decades. For instance, in 1985 the total value of Turkish exports to the ROK was around $3.6 million, but the Turks imported $28.8 million of Korean products.[338] In 2018, the two-way trade between them amounted to

---

[334] "Interview: Turkey Hails China's 1st Import Expo, Gets Ready for Next Session: Minister," *Xinhua*, November 30, 2018.

[335] "Japan, Turkey Open Trade Talks in Tokyo," *The Japan Times*, December 1, 2014.

[336] "Turkey Expects to Sign Free Trade Deal with Japan in H1 2019, Minister Says," *Reuters*, November 14, 2018.

[337] "Taiwan Eyeing Turkey as Springboard to Middle East Trade," *Taiwan Focus*, July 22, 2013; "CEOs of 250 Japanese Giants to Build Ties with Turkish Industrialists," *Daily Sabah*, September 6, 2018; and "Japan and Turkey Seek Early Conclusion of Free Trade Accord," *The Japan Times*, September 25, 2018.

[338] "South Korea Looks for Deeper Economic Ties with Turkey," *Daily Sabah*, July 31, 2018; and "Turkey, Korea Deepen Future-oriented Cooperation," *Korea Herald*, November 5, 2018.

$7.2 billion, including some $6 billion of South Korean exports to Turkey and $1.2 billion of Turkish exports to the ROK.[339]

Moreover, many Korean contractors are engaged in major construction projects in Turkey, including the Canakkale Bridge which is going to be the longest suspension bridge in the world. This prominent undertaking is scheduled to be completed in 2023. Before a significant depreciation of the Turkish lira in 2018 and the ensuing economic turmoil in the country, the Turks had had high expectations for 2023, which marks the 100th anniversary of the establishment of the Republic of Turkey. In fact, Turkey's "Vision 2023" plan is inspired in part by this important milestone, as the nation aims to emerge as one of the top 10 economies in the world by that year.

Having achieved an economic growth record of around 9 percent in 2010 and 8.5 percent in 2011, such a rosy forecast and attention-getting projects indubitably motivated some of Turkey's Asian partners such as the Japanese and especially the Koreans to expedite their FAT negotiations with Ankara in anticipation of the economic opportunities that would naturally flow from an emerging market transforming into a top-10 economy.[340] And while the recent economic tumult may dampen their progress for a time, Turkey is still going to remain among the top 20 economies in the world, and it remains a coveted location for Asian businesses, including those in Taiwan and India.[341]

Turkey's expanding commercial relations with Asian nations certainly would have done a lot better, however, if significant progress had come about to some highly ambitions projects and landmark deals which the AKP-led Turkish governments had negotiated over years with their Eastern

---

[339] Retrospectively, the volume of bilateral trade between Turkey and South Korea was roughly $16,000 in 1965. "New Deal to Boost Trade Volume between S. Korea, Turkey," *Hurriyet Daily News*, February 18, 2019.

[340] "Turkey Rattles the Global Economy," *The Japan Times*, August 16, 2018; and "China Reiterates Support for Turkey's Economy," *Middle East Monitor*, August 19, 2018.

[341] While Turkey and India expect their two-way trade reach $10 billion by 2020, commercial interactions between the Turks and their Taiwanese counterparts are more consequential. In spite of its unwavering attachment to the "one-China policy," Turkey has long engaged in varied economic, financial, technological, and cultural interactions with Taiwan. Many Taiwanese companies have also thrown their capital and technical know-how into different Turkish projects. It is an important objective for Taiwan to eventually conclude a FTA with Turkey. Like its East Asian rivals, moreover, Taiwan regularly enjoys trade surplus with Turkey. In 2017, for instance, the total two-way trade between Ankara and Taipei valued around $1.7 billion, including some $300 million for Turkey's exports to Taiwan and the rest for Taiwanese exports to Turkey. "Turkey: Trade with India will Reach $10bn by 2020," *Middle East Monitor*, August 3, 2018; "Taiwan–Turkey Business Council to be Held in May," *The China Post*, May 2, 2014; "Taiwan Eyeing Russia, Turkey to Boost Exports," *Taiwan Focus*, June 14, 2014; "Taiwan Cement to Invest $1.1bn in New Turkey Joint Venture," *Nikkei Asian Review*, October 27, 2018; and "'Turkey is on Taiwan's Radar': Representative," *Anadolu Agency*, October 20, 2018.

partners.[342] A case in point is a pivotal nuclear power project signed in 2013 between Turkey and a Japan-led consortium. The plan was to build a nuclear plant for the Turks in the Sinop area along the Black Sea coast. The lead builder, Mitsubishi Heavy Industries LTD, however, surprisingly abandoned the contract in 2018, on the grounds that the project was no longer financially feasible because the costs turned out to be double the initial forecast.[343] Another vital nuclear power plant project, a high priority partnership between Turkey and the ROK, was initiated in 2010, but due to unspecified financial and technological impediments this potentially lucrative deal, estimated to be worth around $20 billion, also fell through. Still, the two countries vowed to maintain their cooperation on different aspects of nuclear power energy.[344]

Cultural springboard

As a nation of people who originally migrated from Central Asia, the Turks have certainly had considerable cultural connections to the East over the centuries. And despite Turkey's more recent enthusiastic quest to learn Western ways of doing things, the country never meant to cut off from the Eastern countries with their common bonds and shared values.[345] Turkey became a successful combination of Eastern and Western cultures, giving it a unique identity.[346] Under the AKP, moreover, many Turks were no longer shy to show off their Eastern mores by highlighting traditional norms and symbols which Turkey shares with many Eastern societies. The outcome was sometimes rather sensational when such conduct and manners involved high-profile figures in the AKP or immediate members of their families. This proud emphasis on Turkey's commonalities with the East made the country more popular with many Middle Eastern and Asian countries.[347]

---

[342] "Gov't to Give up Plan to Export Nuclear Power Reactors to Turkey," *The Mainichi,* January 4, 2019.

[343] "Japan to Scrap Turkey Nuclear Project," *Nikkei Asian Review,* December 4, 2018; and "Japan Dropping Nuclear Plant Export to Turkey over Rising Costs," *The Asahi Shimbun,* December 6, 2018.

[344] "Turkey, South Korea Sign Major Trade Deal," *Hurriyet Daily News,* June 9, 2014; and "Korea–Turkey Relations," *Korea Times,* May 14, 2018.

[345] Carter V. Findley, *The Turks in World History* (New York: Oxford University Press, 2005), p. 27; and David Lawday, "Turkey Aims to be a Middle East Japan," *U.S. News & World Report,* Vol. 111, No. 5 (July 29, 1991), p. 36.

[346] Martin Stokes, *The Republic of Love: Cultural Intimacy in Turkish Popular Music* (Chicago and London: The University of Chicago Press, 2010), pp. 23, 149.

[347] Laurence Raw, *Exploring Turkish Cultures: Essays, Interviews and Reviews* (Newcastle upon Tyne, UK: Cambridge Scholars Publishing, 2011), p. 258.

In addition to making a meaningful increase in formal academic and non-academic cultural exchanges with Asia, Turkey now paid special attention to the tourism sector and managed to attract a surprising number of travelers from Eastern nations. The Turks had already taken advantage of this asset with regard to a great part of their neighboring regions. In 2019, for instance, the number of international tourists visiting Turkey climbed to over 52 million, a significant number of whom arrived from Russia, Iran, Georgia, Ukraine, Iraq, Azerbaijan, Greece, and Israel. Now it was time for Turkey to make most of surging East and South Asian sightseers and excursionists. Despite some fluctuations due to political issues and security matters, tourism remained a major export sector for Turkey, accounting for some one-fifth of all goods and services exported. This further encouraged the country to focus on the East in order to sustain its thriving tourism and service exports. In addition, the projected decline in tourism from the West could be offset significantly by attracting visitors from the East, as projections suggested they might see at least one million tourists from China and India alone.[348]

Chinese and Indian tourists were not the only promising targets, however. Turkey drafted some new measures which could open the door to more vacationers from large and from smaller countries.[349] One effective approach was to abolish the mandatory visa system with some Asian countries; in other cases reciprocal free e-visa agreements were signed.[350] Moreover, the national air carrier, Turkish Airlines, and other airline companies were encouraged to establish new routes across Asia.[351] Since metropolitan Istanbul is connected to at least fifty European cities alone, this provided an important transit point and gateway to the rest of the world, offering affordable onward routes for many tourists and business people from Central Asia

---

[348] "Turkey Aims to Woo 1 mln Chinese to Save Declining Tourism this Year," *Xinhua*, May 15, 2016; and "200,000 Chinese Tourists Expected to Visit Turkey in 2017," *Middle East Monitor*, September 11, 2017.

[349] With the blessing of successive AKP governments, Turkey also became a hive of cultural activity for a host of Asian philanthropists and non-governmental organizations (NGOs) assisting a swarm of Iraqi and Syrian refugees sheltered by the Turks. Suzy Hansen, "The Erdogan Loyalists and the Syrian Refugees," *The New York Times*, July 20, 2016; "Taiwanese Businessmen Donate 10,000 Coats, Boots to Refugees in Turkey's Kilis," *Daily Sabah*, February 10, 2017; and "Japan-funded Facility for Syrian Refugee Women Opens in Turkey," *The Japan Times*, November 9, 2017.

[350] "Turkey—Brother Nation of Korea," *Korea Times*, November 15, 2015; and "Taiwan and Turkey Sign Reciprocal Free E-visas Agreement to Boost Tourism," *The China Post*, February 3, 2016.

[351] "Turkish Airlines Launches New Route to Taiwan," *Anadolu Agency*, March 31, 2015; and "Beijing Issues Travel Warning after Turkey Protests Target Chinese," *CNN*, July 6, 2015.

---

and eastern Asia.[352] Turkey also offered full-service wedding packages and a range of health care services up to and including surgery, capitalizing on all aspects of foreign tourism to create more jobs and increase the national income by boosting the service sector.[353]

Conclusion

Turkey had jumped through hoops for decades, struggling to align itself more closely with Western countries and demonstrating its willingness to follow the security and foreign policies required by its commitment to key institutions in the West such as NATO. Even Turkey's foreign economic and cultural policies were influenced by the country's intention to join the West through a formal membership in the European Union. The ascendency of the AKP Islamists in 2002, however, made the Turks reappraise their foreign policy priorities.

Of course, Turkey did not abandon its security alliance with the West, nor did it give up the long-cherished goal of becoming a member of the EU. But the Turks recognized that they did not really have to look for their holy grail in the West alone. They realized they would do better to diversify their foreign alliances by building strong relationships with some of the new centers of wealth and power, in particular by looking East.

The Turkish looking-East approach amounted to bringing the country's new political and strategic identity into line with its growing economic and technological interests. Under Erdoğan, Turkey was certainly sincere in its belated return to the East and manifested this interest by fostering closer ties with almost every Asian country. The political rhetoric and official position of many AKP leaders about regional and international matters showed that the ruling Islamists had much in common with many of their Eastern counterparts. But beyond politics, Turkey was also counting on satisfying its growing economic, financial, and technical needs through partnerships in the East. The Turks were willing to sacrifice some of their politico-ideological and cultural commitments from time to time, in the hope of securing their growing business expectations in the East, as was demonstrated by the ups and downs in Turkish–Chinese relations.[354] After all, the AKP leadership

---

[352] "Taiwan Upbeat about Direct Flight Accord with Turkey," *The China Post*, December 26, 2014; and "Maiden flight from Turkey Arrives in Taiwan," *Taiwan Focus*, March 31, 2015.

[353] "Young Turkish People are Interested in Korean Culture," *Korea Times*, December 4, 2017; "Anwar's Shoulder Surgery in Turkey a Success," *The Straits Times*, July 13, 2018; and "'2019 to be Year of Turkish Culture in Japan'," *Anadolu Agency*, November 4, 2018.

[354] "Is Turkey 'Gravitating' Toward China? — Analysis," *Eurasia Review*, April 6, 2014; "Turkey Promises to Eliminate Anti-China Media Reports," *Reuters*, August 3, 2017; "China, Turkey Should Maintain High-level Exchanges, Deepen Strategic Mutual Trust:

had to constantly make painful adjustments in order to continue to main-tain their legitimacy in the eyes of the now anxious secularists and Western-oriented sectors in Turkey.

By the same token, many Asian countries seemed eager to do business with Turkey. Turkey's partial detachment from the West was regarded as a significant victory for the East, and the country's critical location and demographic size looked promising for the Asian countries' own plans for expanding their political and economic interests. The Turks obviously had a lot to offer, particularly to China and India with their expanding inter-ests all around the countries and regions bordering Turkey. For the Chinese, Turkey was an indispensable link in their newly-announced plan to recreate the ancient Silk Road, while other major Asian economies moved to exploit promising Turkish markets for their products. Even smaller economies in the ASEAN region, those with a poor record of ties with Turkey in the past, engaged in higher volume of interactions with Ankara, aiming to capitalize on its location as a literal bridge between Asia and Europe and neighboring regions.

Xi," *Global Times*, April 20, 2018; and "Chinese, Turkish FMs Meet for Closer Cooperation," *Global Times*, September 28, 2018.

CHAPTER 6. ISRAEL: SWIMMING WITH THE TIDE

Israel is often perceived to be a bastion of the West in the heart of the Middle East. The Israeli Western-style liberal democracy is also thought to differ from the authoritarian systems and half-baked democracies which predominate throughout the region. Because of the nature of its political institutions and social values, the country is sometimes looked on as an integral part of the West. More importantly, the Israeli state has been in very close alliance with Western countries, Britain and the United States in particular, which were instrumental in the establishment of today's Israel in Palestine in the late 1940s. This has given the West a predominant role in Israel's decision-making with regard to security, diplomatic, economic, and even cultural policies. Of course, almost all Western governments have been sympathetic to the Israelis during the past seven decades, pledging umpteen times to uphold the special relationship with the Jewish state as a cornerstone of their broader policies toward the region.[355]

However, while its close affinity and peculiar partnership with the West has persisted for many decades, Israel has in recent years embarked upon a looking-East approach in earnest. In the words of the incumbent prime minister and a principal architect of the country's looking-East policy, Israel has chosen to pivot toward Asia in a "very clear and purposeful way."[356] From giving similarly clear-cut statements on multiple occasions to taking a whole host of bold steps toward Asian nations, the Israeli leadership has left little

---

[355] Jonathan Adelman, *The Rise of Israel: A History of a Revolutionary State* (Abingdon and New York: Routledge, 2008), p. 77.
[356] "Israel is Clearly Pivoting to Asia, Netanyahu Announces in Singapore," *The Jerusalem Post*, February 21, 2017.

doubt about its looking-East resolve. Even prior to this new drive, the Israelis had certainly initiated and maintained bilateral relations with many Asian countries in different areas favorable to them. They succeeded particularly in commencing mutually beneficial relations with a number of Asian powers since the early 1990s. The new looking-East orientation is, however, more inclusive, encompassing more countries and more spheres of collaboration.

Given its unique tie-in with the West, what compelled Israel to look East in the first place? Since the Israelis have fostered deep and durable connections to all powerful countries in the West for as long as it has existed, and can always count on their support, did they really need to curry favor with Asian nations? Which imperatives convinced Israel to formulate such a new policy? Moreover, what are the essential characteristics of the Israeli looking-East concept? Do they differ significantly from the approaches taken by other countries in the region? How about Israel's partners in the East? Were they really prepared to move beyond certain complicated matters that had tested their bilateral ties in the past and engage the Israelis afresh?

Tapping into the zeitgeist: The Israeli version of looking East

Israel is historically an Asian nation regardless of the fact that its contemporary identity is made up of both oriental and occidental elements. The religion of the Jews as well as many of their sacred places all have Asian identification. Many well-known Jewish traditions and customs are identified more with Eastern than Western societies. Moreover, Jews of non-Western origin form the very fabric of modern Israeli society, though a significant number of the people who founded the modern Jewish state were born in a Western country.[357] In fact, since the establishment of Israel in May 1948, a large proportion of its naturalized citizens have emigrated from Eastern countries, a trend that is going to continue for the foreseeable future. These Jewish immigrants often maintain connections with the Eastern society they left behind. It is also more likely that this expanding group of Israeli inhabitants will display cultural mores which are considered typical of an Eastern rather than Western society.[358]

In the face of all those critical commonalities which Israel shares with the East, however, the looking-East approach was not meant to be a quest to

---

[357] Surprisingly, when Israel was founded in 1948, the country formally adopted a perplexing policy of non-identification with either the East or the West. For more details, see: Colin Shindler, *A History of Modern Israel*, second edition (New York: Cambridge University Press, 2013), p. 110.

[358] David Tal, ed., *Israeli Identity: Between Orient and Occident* (Abingdon and New York: Routledge, 2013); and Gregory S. Mahler, *Politics and Government in Israel: The Maturation of a Modern State* (Lanham, MD: Rowman & Littlefield, 2011), p. 77.

return to its roots. Quite to the contrary, it seems that the Israelis are more adamant about their deeper integration into the West than their identification with the East. Israel has always counted on the West to protect it in its isolated position in the Middle East. The country would hardly be willing to forego such support for the sake of fostering new ties to the East. After all, their very survival requires reliable close relations with those powerful and determined Western countries which regard the defense of the Jewish state as a priority. Israel's technological leaps and long term economic prosperity would also oblige the country to team up with the West, even while it wants to act as a bridge of sorts between the East and the West.[359]

Israel's looking-East orientation did not come into play primarily as a bargaining chip in the aftermath of political frictions between Israel and its Western (and especially European) allies. It's true that a number of anti-Israeli measures, such as boycotting its products and services by some Western groups and political activists, could potentially tarnish the country's international image; however, a looking-East push would not pressure those non-state entities to moderate their anti-Israeli rhetoric.[360] Nor could the looking-East approach really be interpreted as a "strategic hedge" vis-à-vis Western governments, even if some Israeli politicians and thinkers foresaw that the economic and political power of the East was inevitably moving ahead. Israel's dependence on the West is too profound to be safeguarded simply by creating an insurance policy in Asia.[361]

The true nature of Israel's looking-East push is, therefore, mostly about the huge economic potential which derives from developing better relations with Asian countries. Although the West still accounts for the bulk of Israel's commercial interactions with the outside world, the rise of the East has provided the Israelis with large economic gains. In this sense, the Israelis are simply following a trend in the Middle East and around the globe. Just as many Arab allies of the West had individually inaugurated their own looking-East orientations, Israel became more inclined to build better connections to Asia. Of course, not all the Middle East states have identical motivations to Israel's when it comes to looking-East, but the economic aspects are paramount in most cases.

---

[359] David Pollock, "Israel's National Unity: Solution or Stalemate?" in Robert Owen Freedman, ed., *The Middle East from the Iran-Contra Affair to the Intifada* (New York: Syracuse University Press, 1991), pp. 207–233.
[360] "Israel in Asia? Why Global Trends are Pushing Israel to 'Look East'," *Stroum Center for Jewish Studies*, April 25, 2018.
[361] James F. Petras, *The Power of Israel in the United States* (Atlanta: Clarity Press, 2006); and John J. Mearsheimer & Stephen M. Walt, "Is It Love or the Lobby? Explaining America's Special Relationship with Israel," *Security Studies*, Vol. 18, No. 1 (2009), pp. 58–78.

Meanwhile, many Asian countries were enthusiastic about engaging the Jewish state. In sharp contrast to those days when Asians were reticent about establishing relations with Israel, more and more governments and companies from the East have flocked to the country in recent years to promote their business interests among the Israelis. And just as the Asians are no longer reserved about establishing connections to the Jewish state, the Israelis also appear to be less obsessed about their "recognition and acceptance" by Eastern societies.[362] While engaging each other, the two sides have sometimes even raised some highly contentious political issues or cooperated on non-economic matters, but their chief concern indubitably remains the pursuit of tangible economic and financial benefits. In particular, the rationale for Israel's looking-East approach is missed or misinterpreted when the media emphasize Israel's non-economic stakes in Asia.[363]

Politico-strategic elements: Shifting priorities

The nature and scope of Israel's political and strategic relationship with the East underwent a seismic change after the end of the Cold War and the disappearance of the Soviet Union from world politics.

More importantly, it was the ensuing peace process between the Israelis and Palestinians that opened the pathway for Israel to gradually normalize its diplomatic interactions with some of the more powerful and influential countries throughout Asia. Prior to that promising period, Israel had remained very isolated in the Mideast for most of its existence, since Israel's treatment of the Palestinians made Arab-friendly Asian nations think twice

---

[362] Arturo Marzano, "The Loneliness of Israel. The Jewish State's Status in International Relations," *The International Spectator*, Vol. 48, No. 2 (2013), pp. 96–113.

[363] There has been, however, some highly political issues in Israel's relationship with the East, supplying grist to the mills of world's media and press to often give prominence to the role of non-economic matters involving the two sides or a third party. Iran, for instance, turned out to be a hot-button issue in Israel's interactions especially with more powerful and resourceful Asian nations, as the Israelis worked relentlessly to take advantage of their growing ties with Eastern countries in order to put additional pressures on Tehran, primarily through economic sanctions and political isolation, over its nuclear program and Middle Eastern policies. The Israelis even appealed to small political entities in Asia such as Taiwan to seriously reconsider their ongoing economic and technological cooperation with the Iranians. In particular, Benjamin Netanyahu used to make overtures about the graveness of the Iranian threat while meeting his Asian counterparts here and there. For more details, see: Roger Howard, "Why Israel Fears an Iranian Bomb," *The RUSI Journal*, Vol. 150, No. 1 (2008), pp. 65–69; Haggai Ram, *Iranophobia: The Logic of an Israeli Obsession* (Stanford, CA: Stanford University Press, 2009); and Albert B. Wolf, "After the Iran Deal: Competing Visions for Israel's Nuclear Posture," *Comparative Strategy*, Vol. 35, No. 2 (2016), pp. 124–130.

about showing any overt sympathy for the Israelis.[364] By the time the Jewish state embarked upon a looking-East orientation in earnest, therefore, many Asian countries were no longer used to looking at Israel as a pariah and an outcast "garrison state" in the Middle East. The history of Israeli international socialization was now certainly longer in the West than in the East, but this limitation would not really hinder Israel and its recent Eastern partners in moving past their erstwhile political grievances and conflicting strategic calculations. The two sides were adamant about taking care of their new interests.[365]

China is, again, the most important Eastern nation which became a target of the looking-East approach. There had been ups and downs in Sino–Israeli connections before. Despite the fact that Israel was one of the first non-communist countries to recognize Mao's China in September 1950, Beijing was steadfastly attached to its formulaic pro-Palestinian thinking, inimical to the Israelis for a couple of decades to come. Maoist China was not shy about demonizing Israel as an "agent of imperialism" installed by the West in the Middle East.[366] In sharp contrast to this idealistic (and rancorous) attitude prior to the normalization of ties between the two countries, however, China adopted over time a more realistic policy vis-à-vis Israel.[367]

Of course, the Chinese still continued to display a semblance of their pro-Arab inclinations and even offered time and again to mediate as an honest broker between the Israelis and Palestinians, but such moves may be seen as tokenistic and having more to do with preserving China's expanding interests simultaneously in Israel and Muslim countries in the Middle East and beyond.[368] This new Chinese pragmatism obviously gave a boost to the Israeli looking-East drive, even if many countries still did not construe it as a *volte-face* in China's overall approach toward the region.

Compared to China, other important and resourceful Asian countries proved to be easier for the Israelis to court. Some, such as Japan and South Korea, were, for instance, close allies of the United States with a great deal of identical security and foreign policy preferences. In spite of its half-hearted

---

[364] Michael Walzer, *A Foreign Policy for the Left* (New Haven and London: Yale University Press, 2018), p. 52.

[365] Christopher L. Schilling, *Emotional State Theory: Friendship and Fear in Israeli Foreign Policy* (Lanham, MD: Lexington Books, 2018), p. 88.

[366] Charles D. Freilich, *Zion's Dilemmas: How Israel Makes National Security Policy* (Ithaca and London: Cornell University Press, 2012), p. 69.

[367] "China 'Devastated' by Continuing Palestine–Israel Conflict: FM," *Xinhua*, July 29, 2014; and "Are China and Japan the New Peace Process Mediators?" *The Jerusalem Post*, December 27, 2017.

[368] Adam Garfinkle, *Politics and Society in Modern Israel: Myths and Realities*, second edition (New York and London: M.E. Sharpe, 2000), p. 210.

quarterbacking for the Arab cause, Japan was essentially the first Asian country to recognize the state of Israel in May 1952, and Tokyo later engaged in a closer and more complementary relationship with the Israelis since the mid-1980s onward.[369] The Republic of Korea turned out to be less willing than Japan to demonstrate overt friendship with Israel, but Seoul's cautious approach was related to its sense of susceptibility vis-à-vis the Arabs. Over the past several years, therefore, Japanese leaders became less skittish to embrace their Israeli counterparts and did so frequently and publicly, whereas the Koreans often preferred to engage Israel more in economic and technological fields than in loud and eye-catching political displays.[370]

Unlike Japan and the ROK, India was a somewhat harder nut to crack. True, India is also a friend and ally of the United States, but the Indians had a rocky relationship with the Israelis prior to the normalization of diplomatic ties in 1992. In fact, India's standoffish attitude had to do with its proactive membership in the Non-Aligned Movement as well as the role of the Muslim minority within the Indian society.[371] Even after the Indians agreed to normalize diplomatic ties with the Jewish state in the early 1990s, they behaved prudently and abstained from expressing publicly any strong solidarity with the Israelis. Dovetailing nicely with the Israeli looking-East drive, however, the Indian policy toward Israel seems to be changing, albeit quietly. Like their Chinese rivals, the Indians have become increasingly cognizant of their long-term economic and technological interests in Israel, compelling them to opt for more realistic and businesslike measures.[372]

Meanwhile, with its looking-East approach Israel also sought to benefit from better interactions with smaller players in the Association of Southeast Asian Nations. The Israelis had actually maintained official diplomatic ties with the ASEAN members Myanmar (Burma) and Singapore since 1953 and 1969, respectively, and even some recent human rights issues in Myanmar did not put a stop to Israel's good relations with that country.[373] Of course, other ASEAN members such as Indonesia and especially Malaysia still refused vehemently to reappraise their attitude toward Israel, but nothing discouraged the Filipinos from welcoming the Israelis with open arms.[374]

---

[369] Jacob Abadi, *Israel's Quest for Recognition and Acceptance in Asia: Garrison State Diplomacy* (London: Frank Cass Publishers, 2004), p. 97.

[370] Abadi, 124; and "Japan, Israel Upgrade Relations as Arab Oil Influence Wanes," *Reuters*, September 5, 2016.

[371] Freilich, p. 57.

[372] Nicolas Blarel, "Assessing US Influence over India–Israel Relations: A Difficult Equation to Balance?" *Strategic Analysis*, Vol. 41, No. 4 (2017), pp. 384–400.

[373] "Israel Retains Warm Ties with Myanmar despite Human Rights Issues," *Haaretz*, February 5, 2019.

[374] "Malaysia not Alone in Boycotting Israel," *New Straits Times*, February 13, 2019.

In September 2018, Rodrigo Duterte became the first Filipino president to embark upon an official visit to Israel since the two countries had established their diplomatic relations in 1957.[375] In the same way, Lee Hsien Loong became the first Singaporean prime minister who made a state visit to Israel in April 2016 to get in on the Israeli "pivot to the East."[376]

Growing military connections

The military plays an indispensable role in Israel, wielding enormous influence over aspects of the social, political and economic affairs of the country. Israel is a security state; from its inception it has relied on its military in order to survive. The prominent role of the military has not faded over time, because the Jewish state has had to perpetually grapple with its special circumstances. The critical role of the military was never constrained to domestic politics, either; foreign affairs have also been influenced significantly by an array of advisory services and policy recommendations that trickle down through the military establishment.[377] Moreover, a great number of Israeli leaders and policymakers come from the military ranks, bringing with them many years of knowledge and experience gleaned through working as army officers. In any case, a wide consensus within the Israeli society over the principle of civilian control of the military has remained by and large unchallenged.[378]

As a corollary to that, the military has created its own relevant industries, some of which constitute a pillar of the country's national economy. Thanks to its technical knowhow and sophistication in the arms industry, Israel eventually emerged as a major arms dealer and an exporter of munitions. Thus it is natural that the military industry expects the people and institutions in charge of Israel's foreign affairs to do their own heavy lifting by creating the conditions for broader military cooperation and arms trade with the outside world. Still, the military industry was hardly ever a liability for the country's diplomacy because the strength in armaments became a crucial asset, giving Israel an edge while conducting its foreign and commercial interactions with many other nations. Far from being a chink in its diplomatic armor, therefore, Israel's accomplishments in military equipment and

---

[375] After all, the Philippines was the only Asian country which voted in favor of UN Resolution 181 that led to the creation of the state of Israel.

[376] "In First Visit ever by Singapore PM, Leader Thanks Israel for Defense Aid over the Years," *The Jerusalem Post*, April 18, 2016.

[377] Patrick Tyler, *Fortress Israel: The Inside Story of the Military Elite Who Run the Country — and Why They Can't Make Peace* (New York: Farrar, Straus and Giroux, 2012), pp. 8–9.

[378] Charles D. Freilich, "Can Israel Survive Without America?" *Survival*, Vol. 59, No. 4 (2017), pp. 135–150; and Mahler, p. 200.

training have boosted its diplomacy, contributing to the building of inter-national connections in varied military and non-military fields as well.[379] Likewise, the Israeli looking-East approach could both serve the military industry and benefit from its strength.

However, despite the fact that Israel maintained robust military interac-tions with the West, especially the United States, its exports of arms and munitions to North America and European countries gradually plummeted, forcing the country to ramp up its arms marketing in the rising East.[380] Many Asian countries were already allocating huge portions of their budgets for defense programs and military purchases, an opportunity the Israelis quickly tapped into. By the time Israel got serious about looking East, the country was exporting to Asia close to 60 percent of its defense products, ranging from small unmanned aerial vehicles (UAVs) to large tanks. The East had emerged, therefore, as the largest market for Israeli military products, and now the looking-East policy could further exploit this development to both secure the military industry's competitive edge and promote the country's ties with agreeable Asian nations in other economic sectors.[381]

Of course, Israel had a long history of military deals with Asian countries, harkening back to 1954 when Myanmar became the first nation to purchase obsolete Spitfire aircraft from the Jewish state. More than one decade before the official Sino–Israeli political relationship was commenced, Israel had engaged in quiet yet significant military relations with China. And despite a lack of formal diplomatic ties, Israel became an important arms partner of Taiwan, supplying Taipei with significant volumes of military equipment, mostly clandestinely, albeit with tacit American approval and support.[382] In the same way, some other smaller Asian countries such as Singapore benefited greatly from Israel's military exports. In more recent years, many Eastern nations, from South Korea and Vietnam to China and India, all have demonstrated a keen desire to engage in arms deals and military cooperation with Israel.[383] They have been keen to buy advanced weaponry from Israel

---

[379] Garfinkle.

[380] Blaine D. Holt, "The Gold Standard: U.S.–Israel Military Relations," *American Foreign Policy Interests*, Vol. 36, No. 2 (2014), pp. 111–118.

[381] "Japan, Israel to Boost Defense Cooperation," *The Japan Times*, May 12, 2014; "Korea, Israel Teaming up on Drones," *Korea Joongang Daily*, June 21, 2016; and "Philippines' Duterte Eyes Arms Deals on Israel Trip," *Bangkok Post*, September 2, 2018.

[382] Jonathan Goldstein, "The Republic of China and Israel," in Jonathan Goldstein, ed., *China and Israel, 1948–1998: A Fifty Year Retrospective* (London: Praeger, 1999), pp. 1–35.

[383] Adam Segal, "Chinese Economic Statecraft and the Political Economy," in William W. Keller, and Thomas G. Rawski, eds., *China's Rise and the Balance of Influence in Asia* (Pittsburgh, PA: University of Pittsburgh Press, 2007), pp. 146–161.

at a fair cost and to enter into joint military and defense projects with the Israelis.[384]

Among all of Israel's arms deals with the East, however, none of them turned out to be more controversial than Israel's military cooperation with China.[385] The controversy actually dates back to separate cases in the late 1990s and mid-2000s when the United States objected to some impending military agreements involving Israel and China, forcing the Israelis to eventually and grudgingly cancel these lucrative deals with the Chinese.[386] Perceiving China as a long-term strategic rival and a force menacing its hegemonic position in the Asia–Pacific region, the Americans view any Chinese military cooperation with Israel as a backdoor through which the rising East Asian power can gain access to American military technologies and potentially undermine its security at home and abroad.[387] Still, in spite of Israel's obligation to heed any requests put forward by the United States, including making painful cutbacks in its defense deals and military cooperation with Beijing, the Chinese have persevered to preserve their cooperation with the Israelis in other critical fields, especially the transfer of non-military technologies.

Technology transfer: Fast-tracking the modus operandi

Since the 1960s, Israel has exploited technology transfers as an effective tool to promote its strategic, political, and economic interests. Serving its political and non-political interests simultaneously, the transfer of technology has also enabled the Jewish state to influence its recipient countries to adjust some of their policy behaviors in lockstep with Israeli interests and expectations. As a knowledge economy, and despite its own peculiar shortcomings and limitations, Israel has thereby taken advantage of its innovative and entrepreneurial image in the world in order to accelerate the Israeli looking-East program among Asian countries.[388] Undoubtedly, a lot of major

---

[384] "S. Korea Pushes to Buy 10 Low-altitude Radars from Israel," *Yonhap New Agency*, April 9, 2014; "South Korea Eyeing Israeli Rocket Interceptor - Manufacturer," *Reuters*, August 10, 2014; and "India Largest Purchaser of Israel Arms in 2017," *Middle East Monitor*, May 4, 2018.

[385] Yitzhak Shichor, "Israel's Military Transfers to China and Taiwan," *Survival*, Vol. 40, No. 1 (1998), pp. 68–91; and Christopher L. Schilling, "The Problem of Romanticising Israel–Taiwan Relations," *Israel Affairs*, Vol. 24, No. 3 (2018), pp. 460–466.

[386] Freilich, p. 310; and Michael B. Oren, *Ally: My Journey across the American–Israeli Divide* (New York: Random House, 2015), p. 178.

[387] "Companies behind Israel's Iron Dome Hacked by China: Report," *Newsweek*, July 29, 2014; and "China is Spying on Israel to Steal U.S. Secrets," *Foreign Policy*, March 24, 2019.

[388] David Rosenberg, *Israel's Technology Economy: Origins and Impact* (New York: Palgrave Macmillan, 2018), p. 14.

Israeli companies and start-ups have also displayed a keen desire in recent years to venture into bustling Eastern markets, to compensate for the small size of their domestic markets and make more money. So far, technology transfer has mostly meant taking the technologies and scientific know-how of Israel to the East rather than the other way around, although that could change as the East moves ahead with technologies of its own.[389]

Acknowledging Israel as a country on the leading edge of technologies in the Middle East, therefore, many Asian businesses have worked to create a sort of network facilitating technological collaborations and entrepreneurial activities with their Israeli counterparts.[390] Representatives of both the public and private sectors often perceive Israel as a stepping stone to help their business achieve the high-tech future they are relentlessly seeking.[391] After all, short-term profits as well as the long-term prosperity of many Eastern businesses hinge on constant creativity and innovation, part of which may come through technological partnerships with Israel.[392] Besides purchasing cutting-edge technologies from Israel at a good price, moreover, Asian countries have engaged in collaborative projects with the Israelis in an array of ground-breaking technologies ranging from renewable energies to modern medical equipment. Joint activities in innovative academic and research fields involving Israel and Asian countries are burgeoning as well.[393]

However, the issue of transferring Israeli civilian technologies to the East, just like the issue over military technology, has never been devoid of controversy. While technological ties have always been part and parcel of Israel's relationship with Asian countries over the past several decades, the United States has particularly been very concerned about the problem of reverse engineering, which is widely practiced by some Asian countries.[394]

---

[389] "China, Israel Vow to Push for more Fruitful Innovation Cooperation," *Global Times*, October 26, 2018.

[390] In 2018, for example, China and Israel agreed to upgrade their relationship to a Comprehensive Innovation Partnership. "Israel's Tech Industry is Becoming All About 'China, China, China'," *Bloomberg*, May 29, 2014.

[391] "Israel's Yozma Fund to Invest 1 tln Won in S. Korea," *Yonhap News Agency*, September 1, 2014; and "Taiwan, Israel Seek Further Cooperation on Water Technology," *Taiwan Focus*, November 28, 2014.

[392] "Chinese Business Delegation Comes Tech Shopping in Israel," *The Times of Israel*, March 3, 2012; and "Chinese Investors Flock to Israel for Unlikely Reasons," *The Jerusalem Post*, December 20, 2017.

[393] "Israel Welcomes Tech-hungry Chinese Investors," *Reuters*, May 22, 2014; "Israel's Newest Ally in Asia —Taiwan," *Arutz Sheva*, April 16, 2015; "Hyundai Motor Invests in Israeli Chip Company," *Korean Herald*, July 3, 2018; and "Alibaba's Jack Ma Steals Stage with Speech at Israel Forum," *Global Times*, October 27, 2018.

[394] "Israel's Ties with China are Raising Security Concerns," *The Economist*, October 11, 2018; and "Israel is Being a Bad Ally to the US over China," *Washington Examiner*, December 17, 2018.

Perceiving the matter to be fundamentally incongruent with their own primary national interests, the Americans have also pressed the Israelis to carefully screen and heavily limit the type and scope of the civilian technologies they transfer to Eastern nations, China in particular.[395] The crux of the problem is that giving potential American rivals and adversaries easy access to its technologies and scientific know-how through Israel would enable them to acquire proprietary software and hardware materials, some of which may be used for any non-civilian or sensitive military projects.[396]

A progressive pivot: Widening economic connections

In addition to short-term commercial gains, national economic growth has been a major driving force behind Israel's purposeful and passionate pivot to the East. As an already affluent capitalist system, Israel has set its sights on becoming one of the world's leading 15 economies by taking advantage of the swiftly emerging East.[397] As a case in point, the country's proximity to the Red Sea and Suez Canal would place it virtually at the core of China's highly ambitious Belt and Road Initiative (BRI), providing the Israelis with abundant new investment and commercial possibilities to exploit.

In addition to carving out fresh strategies for increasing its exports to China, moreover, the Jewish state has been equally cognizant of other likely bankable Eastern markets in India, Japan, South Korea, and Singapore.[398] Israel has engaged in serious bilateral negotiations in order to sign separate free trade agreements with a number of promising Asian countries to gain easier and wider access to their up-and-coming markets.

For their part, many Eastern nations, including Vietnam and Taiwan as well as the giants of India and China, have demonstrated a keen desire in fostering closer trade and commercial connections to Israel. In July 2017, for instance, Narendra Modi became the first sitting prime minister of India to visit the Jewish state, in a bid to spur more trade and commercial ties with Israel in spite of their controversial political past. In comparison, however,

---

[395] Recent trade disputes between Washington and Beijing may also drive China toward more high-tech investments in Israel.

[396] Yoram Evron, "Between Beijing and Washington: Israel's Technology Transfers to China," *Journal of East Asian Studies*, Vol. 13, No. 3 (2013), pp. 503–528.

[397] Charles D. Freilich, *Israeli National Security: A New Strategy for an Era of Change* (New York: Oxford University Press, 2018), p. 119.

[398] The money-savvy Israelis have not even ignored the closed and mafia-esque market of North Korea, as they have been tempted to export to the isolated communist state luxury items such as gold despite the lack of any official diplomatic relationship between the two countries and in clear violation of UN sanctions against Pyongyang. "Israel Exported $400,000 of Gold to North Korea Despite UN Sanctions," *Middle East Eye*, December 10, 2015.

India's arch-rival in Asia, China, has been more persistent and successful both in boosting and diversifying its economic and commercial portfolio in Israel.[399]

China is now effectively the second largest trading partner of Israel behind the United States, while Israel's trade with individual European countries is also important. The total volume of two-way trade with China has been ratcheted up to around $15 billion from the small sum of roughly $50 million in 1992, when they normalized their diplomatic relations.[400] Capitalizing on the Israeli looking-East orientation, the Chinese have also significantly supplemented their direct economic investments in Israel, placing themselves in an advantageous position to soon overtake the United States as the number one source of foreign investments in the Jewish state.[401]

Consequently, more than a third of Israel's 15 biggest trading partners are now from the East, accounting for more than a quarter of Israeli imports and exports. Roughly a decade before Israel embarked in earnest upon a looking-East approach, Asia was responsible for some 16 and 19 percent of the country's total imports and exports, respectively.[402] The West still dwarfs the East in terms of its overall share in Israel's foreign trade, but Asia is quickly catching up. More Asian countries are becoming significant partners in Israel's imports and particularly exports. In fact, a key objective of the Israeli looking-East drive has been to boost the share of exports in its foreign trade with Asian nations. The increase in Israeli exports to the East has been particularly fast paced with regard to China and Japan over the past few years. China (including its Special Administrative Region of Hong Kong) is now receiving around 14.5 percent of all Israeli exports compared to a share of some 27 percent for the United States, the largest recipient of Israel's goods and services.[403]

Construction: The Asianization of unskilled labor

As part of its looking-East approach, Israel has not omitted the factor of labor. Asia's large population means it could offer a pool of workers to

---

[399] "Israel and South Korea Could be Economic Powerhouse'," *The Times of Israel*, November 14, 2013; "China to Hold Free Trade Agreement Talks with Israel," *Arutz Sheva*, December 31, 2014; and "Looking East, Israel May Allow More Stock Exchange Dual Listings," *Reuters*, November 2, 2017.

[400] "Chinese Billionaires to Bring their Wallets to Israel," *The Times of Israel*, July 23, 2012.

[401] "Looking East, Israel May Allow More Stock Exchange Dual Listings," *Reuters*, November 2, 2017; "Unlikely Partners? China and Israel Deepening Trade Ties," *BBC*, July 19, 2018; and "Israel–China Ties Are a Very Good Thing," *Haaretz*, October 22, 2019.

[402] Mahler, p. 91; and Cameron G. Thies, *The United States, Israel, and the Search for International Order: Socializing States* (Abingdon and New York: Routledge, 2013), p. 103.

[403] Data taken from *The Central Bureau of Statistics* (Israel) available at: https://www.cbs.gov.il/.

animate Israel's booming construction industry. The policy of bringing in foreign workers dates back, by and large, to the late 1990s when the Israeli government decided to replace Palestinian laborers with workers from other countries and regions, for security as well as economic reasons. By the time the Jewish state formulated its looking-East approach, a number of Asian countries were already showing themselves to be attractive options, both for importing manual laborers and commissioning professional contractors. In fact, since the first oil shock of 1973, Asian contractors had secured a leading role in the construction industry of many Middle Eastern countries, providing high-quality, affordable and timely project completion, primarily using their own workforce. It was high time for Israel, too, to bring in Asian contractors and unskilled workers. This enabled the country to implement its swiftly growing infrastructure projects worth tens of billions of dollars, in both the public and private sectors.[404]

It is estimated that currently more than half of foreign workers in Israel come from Asian countries, including the Philippines, Thailand, Nepal, India, Sri Lanka, and especially China. Such manual laborers are assigned primarily to construction, agricultural, and nursing jobs.[405] A milestone, moreover, was reached in September 2015 when Israel signed an agreement with China to bring in nearly 20,000 Chinese workers, an astonishing number, to engage in construction schemes in Israel, excluding projects in the West Bank or East Jerusalem, 36 of which Israel had earmarked for the Chinese.[406] A number of hard-charging construction companies from China were also offered new contracts to enlarge Israel's two crucial ports in Haifa and Ashdod, which handle the bulk of the country's trade with the outside world. More surprisingly, the Chinese gained the concessions to operate and run the newly constructed harbors for a quarter of a century, provoking many worried voices inside and outside the country to call for barring China from such easy access to what they regard as a "national security asset."[407]

The bottom line is that economic interests, rather than purely security reasons, were a critical factor in allocating massive manual tasks and

---

[404] "Israel Signs Deal to Bring Chinese Laborers, But They Won't Work in West Bank," *The Times of Israel*, April 23, 2017; and "China is Fed up with Israel's Negligence at Construction Sites," *Haaretz*, May 31, 2018.

[405] "61% of Foreign Workers in Israel from Asia," *Khmer Times*, August 1, 2018.

[406] While citing security concerns, the Chinese actually did not want their nationals to get involved in the controversial business of building Jewish settlements, and Israel eventually had to accede to their demand in order to persuade China to sign the deal. The actual number of Chinese workers who later entered Israel fell short of the original estimate of 20,000 people, as well. "Israel Rights Groups Attack Plan to Import 20,000 Chinese Workers," *Financial Times*, September 20, 2015.

[407] "As China Warms up to Israel, Ties Could Cause Security Quandary for the Long-time US Ally," *South China Morning Post*, October 20, 2018.

building projects to Asians by Israel. This was a way to meet election promises delivered by the major political parties with regard to solving the housing crisis and bringing down home prices for the average citizenry. In addition, the Israelis wanted to recruit more Asians because of their lower wage expectations and higher productivity. Since many Asian laborers were able to work at a pace 50 percent more efficient than most of their Israeli and Arab counterparts, Israel could boost its overall national productivity and adeptness by employing Asian laborers and contractors en masse.[408] But one big problem did arise: unskilled foreign workers, Asians in particular, were viewed by Israelis as being at the bottom of the heap and so they were subjected to all sorts of discrimination, including low pay, excessive hours of labor, hazardous working conditions, poor accommodation, passport with-holding, and other human rights matters.[409]

Hard-charging: Making recourse to cultural diplomacy

Aside from capitalizing on techno-economic capabilities which the country possesses, Israel's looking-East approach has been tactical, taking full advantage of public diplomacy to achieve its objectives. Where it comes to exploiting the cultural sinews of publicity and self-promotion, probably few countries have been as hard-charging and successful than the Israelis; and promoting their looking-East objectives among Asian nations was no exception.[410] As a matter of fact, many public institutions in Israel, including the Foreign Ministry and Tourism Ministry, have taken advantage of social media outlets over the past several years, campaigning ardently in order to appeal to their audience across Asia. One important goal has been to enhance Israel's public image among influential intellectuals and public figures, espe-

---

[408] "Chinese Firm Signs Deal as Main Contractor with Israeli Real Estate Company for First Time," *Xinhua*, November 14, 2017; and "Chinese Infrastructure Giants Set Sights on Increased Israel Activity," *The Jerusalem Post*, December 9, 2018.

[409] For instance, Chinese workers were not allowed to frequent brothels or have sexual encounters with Israelis, including prostitutes. This vexing problem sometimes led to illegal trafficking of Chinese women in order to cater to the sexual needs of Chinese men working in Israel. For more details, see: "Chinese Workers in Israel Sign No-sex Contract," *The Guardian*, December 24, 2003; "Chinese Workers Furious at Loss of $1.76 mln," *People's Daily Online*, August 13, 2009; "Trafficking in Persons Report 2011: Country Narratives," *U.S. Department of State*, https://www.state.gov/j/tip/rls/tiprpt/2011/164232. htm; and "Chinese Construction Workers in Israel: Plan to Bring 20,000 from China Criticized by Opponents Who Warn of Labor Exploitation," *International Business Times*, September 21, 2015.

[410] "Israeli PM Benjamin Netanyahu Salutes 'Haven' of Shanghai," *South China Morning Post*, May 7, 2013; and "From China with 'Ahava'," *The Jerusalem Post*, April 14, 2016.

cially in the more powerful and resourceful countries in the East, by applying new means of international communication and information flow.[411]

With regard to more effective practical measures, the cultural diplomacy of Israel in the East has concentrated heavily on the tourism industry. Recognizing the prospective gains to be taken from a growing number of Asian travelers to the Jewish state, the Israeli government has aimed to turn Eastern sightseers and excursionists into cultural ambassadors for Israel. As a critical strategy to tap into that huge potential, many popular Asian stars and celebrities have been approached to play a marketing role among their own fellow citizens back home. In doing so, frequent attempts are made to bring to Israel major movie-making industries in the East, such as India's Bollywood, to produce some of their blockbuster works there.[412] After all, targeting Asian tourists has become more crucial because Israel has designated tourism as a key growth engine. Tourism is currently responsible for some 2.5 percent of the country's gross domestic product (GDP), employing some 200,000 people or roughly 3 percent of the Israeli workforce.[413]

Meanwhile, the Israeli hasbara in the East has hardly been a one-way endeavor, as more and more Asian countries have demonstrated their interest in developing cultural connections to the Jewish state. Asian public and private institutions now seem to be more willing to engage their Israeli counterparts for academic interactions as well as youth and sports exchanges.[414] More Eastern cities have created direct flight routes with Israel, and the conclusion of agreeable visa deals between the Israelis and some Asian nations has reached new heights over the past several years. The perception of Israel has been changing in the East, gradually and favorably, and more Asian governments have embraced pragmatic and viable policies in the area of cultural relations. This evolution in Israeli–Asian cultural ties is exemplified by an increasing number of citations in the East referring to Israel and its contemporary history of nation-building as an illuminating story which Asians can learn from.[415]

---

[411] "Israel Is Looking East," *The Jerusalem Post*, December 17, 2018.
[412] "With Bollywood Glamour and Chinese Stars, Israel Woos Tourists from East," *The Times of Israel*, December 4, 2016.
[413] "Israel Sees Tourism Growth from China, India," *Reuters*, March 31, 2016; and "How Israel is Courting Tourists from India and China," *Jewish Telegraphic Agency*, December 2, 2016.
[414] "Taiwan–Israel Youth Program Ends 7-day Tour," *The China Post*, May 31, 2014; and "An Israeli Lobby in China?" *The Diplomat*, April 30, 2015.
[415] "What We Can Learn from Israelis," *Korea Times*, January 24, 2018.

Conclusion

Over the course of more than seven decades since its creation, Israel's international identity has generally been defined in terms of a close political and security alliance with Western countries, the United States in particular. This sacrosanct principle has wielded significant influence over the dynamics of Israeli domestic affairs. In spite of their ironclad alliance with the West, however, the Israelis have seriously embarked upon a looking-East orientation during the past several years. Aiming to cultivate multifaceted connections to Asian countries, the new Israeli approach is intended to strengthen the Jewish state's relationship with Asia in all political, military, economic, technological, and even cultural areas. Moreover, the looking-East push in Israel has not been a state-driven agenda alone, as the country's thriving private sector has been playing an equally proactive role in developing close interactions with many Asian nations, though the Israeli government has indubitably smoothed the way for larger volumes of relations between the two sides.

But regardless of its salient features, the Israeli looking-East approach is hardly a grand politico-strategic shift in the Jewish state's policy toward the outside world. As late as the conclusion of the Cold War, many countries in the world have come up with their own version of a looking-East initiative, seeking material rewards by forging multifarious ties with the swiftly-growing countries in Asia.

Of course, a number of nations have had their own reasons to go beyond pure economic interests while seeking to develop all-out ties with their Asian counterparts. Israel's "pivot to Asia," however, does not seem to belong to the latter class of master plans in foreign policy which attempt to curry favor with the East at the cost of the West. Like some other nations, the Jewish state is merely striving, albeit belatedly, to make the most of the huge opportunities which Asia's awe-inspiring rise potentially offers. The Israelis will most probably remain committed firmly to their currently propitious alliance in international politics, while pushing persistently for some sort of fresh symbiotic relationship with the East.

Likewise, many countries in Asia have displayed enthusiasm to expand their interactions with Israel, making it much easier for the country to further its objectives among Asians. Some of those Asian nations have actually done an about-turn in their foreign policy toward Israel, mapping out new plans to buttress their presence in the Jewish state. Tempted by Israel's scientific and technological capacities in numerous sectors, this group of Asian countries have encouraged their own public and private companies to take advantage of the country's promise by engaging in higher levels of mutual cooperation with the Israelis. This realistic and pragmatic orientation toward Israel is particularly telling with regard to those Asian powers which keep walking a tight rope in order to secure their substantial interests in the broader Middle East. Such sympathy and reciprocity seem to improve the chances that the Israeli looking-East approach will achieve its main goals.

CHAPTER 7. EGYPT: THE AWAKENING LAGGARD OF LOOKING
EAST

Egypt has a long history of interactions with Asian nations. The modern
record of Egyptian involvement in Asia harkens back at least to the early
1950s when the Arab country was unexpectedly propelled onto the international scene as a result of its championing a quick settlement to the internecine conflict in the Korean Peninsula, which had been exacerbated critically
by the Korean War of 1950–1953. Egypt, in close cooperation with India,
particularly played a mediating role on behalf of the Non-Aligned Movement
in order to resolve the Korean conundrum.[416]

Moreover, Egypt became the first Arab and African country to officially
recognize the communist regime of the People's Republic of China (PRC)
in 1956, and the Middle Eastern nation was then in the midst of developing
close and cordial connections to the communist regime of North Korea as
well.[417] Consequently, Egyptian leaders were among the early Middle East
dignitaries who held high-level meetings with and arranged mutual visits by
their Asian counterparts.

In the face of Egypt's long-established involvement in Asian affairs,
however, the looking-East approach that has been grasped and craved by
some other countries in the region is, in a sense, a new orientation in Egyptian foreign policy. Compared to many other Middle Eastern and North
African countries, Egypt certainly had experiences under its belt in dealing

---

[416] Shirzad Azad, "Iran and the Two Koreas: A Peculiar Pattern of Foreign Policy," *The
Journal of East Asian Affairs*, Vol. 26, No. 2 (fall/winter 2012), pp. 163–192.
[417] Steven A. Cook, *The Struggle for Egypt: From Nasser to Tahrir Square* (New York: Oxford
University Press, 2012), p. 67.

with Eastern nations from the 1950s onward. The Arab country also enjoyed numerous other opportunities to engage in a mutually beneficial relationship with Asia. But it took a long time for the Egyptian government to embark in a more organized way in looking East and to adopt policies and measures in order to achieve some of its new objectives. As it turned out, the Egyptian government was not sufficiently determined about pursuing its new policy goals, nor was its looking-East orientation able to embrace more inclusive strategies and a broader vision with regard to the rapidly changing Asia.

In addition, Egypt emerged as a latecomer of sorts among its fellow Mideast countries, some of which had followed a timely and all-encompassing approach of looking East. As the "first come, first served" rule applies, Egyptians were inevitably in a less favorable position. What most significantly undermined Egypt's ability to promptly adopt a serious policy of looking East, in line with its long record of interactions with many Asian countries? What actually pushed the Egyptian government to come up with such a policy, albeit belatedly? What essentially characterized the Egyptian looking-East drive in the first place, and how does it differ from Cairo's previous experiences of dealing with Asian nations? How about Egypt's counterparts in the East — were Asian nations generally receptive to Egypt? How could they assist Egyptians in fulfilling their new objectives in the East?

Egypt's new approach to the East: Economic imperatives outweigh

The former Egyptian President, Mohamed Morsi, may be generally credited as the architect of Egypt's new looking-East orientation. Morsi won the presidential election in June 2012 with a stronger popular mandate after his affiliated Islamist political group, the Freedom and Justice Party (FJP), had also captured a more number of parliament seats a couple of months earlier. Both Morsi and the FJP had been buttressed by the Muslim Brotherhood which was, and still is, a pivotal political force in Egypt and the oldest Islamist political bloc in the Arab world. With Morsi in the saddle and the Muslim Brotherhood on the march, the commanding heights of Egyptian domestic and especially foreign policy fell unexpectedly into the hands of people who wanted to fundamentally realign Egypt's relationship with the outside world. Morsi's decision to pay his first state visit to China, to the East and not the West, was predicted by many observers to indicate the main focus of a major transformation in Egyptian foreign policy.[418]

---

[418] Chris Zambelis, "A New Egypt Looks to China for Balance and Leverage," *China Brief* (Jamestown Foundation), Vol. 12, No. 18, September 21, 2012.

Traditionally, socialist and left-leaning forces like the FJP and Morsi had shown a propensity for developing closer ties between Egypt and Asian nations. They were at least in favor of allying with non-Western centers of power and influence, no matter if their method of charting a different path in foreign policy was often gradual and incremental. Epitomized by Gamal Abdel Nasser's "positive neutralism," such Egyptian proclivity in foreign policy was to eventually rid the country of menacing foreign presence and interference.[419] After some three and half decades of inconsistency, if not say deviation, from this sacrosanct principle, Morsi and his stalwarts came to devise a new direction in Egyptian foreign policy by favoring closer connections to the East and some other non-Western parts of the world. After all, such a critical transformation in foreign policy by Morsi and his powerful proponents was to ultimately reflect the larger nationalist and populist impulses which had just forced Hosni Mubarak to resign in February 2011 after occupying the domineering office of Egyptian presidency since October 1981.

The Egyptian foreign policy under the Morsi presidency was, therefore, a departure from the system of post-Camp David Accords which dominated the Middle Eastern country's foreign and domestic politics from 1978 until Mubarak's ouster in 2011. Under that alliance system, which was by and large a marriage of convenience, Egypt switched its international allegiance from the Soviet Union to the United States.[420] In exchange for such a major shift in Egypt's grand strategy toward the international pecking order, the Americans provided the Egyptians with tremendous political support as well as more than $60 billion in military, technological, financial, and economic aids over a course of more than three decades. Of course, Egypt did not really compromise its national dignity and independence, but its close collaboration with the West was critical for securing certain vital interests of the United States in the Middle East, including the security of Israel and an uninterrupted sufficient supply of oil from the Persian Gulf region.[421]

Before the Muslim Brotherhood-led visionary politicians make a serious dent in the edifice of Egypt's domestic and foreign policy, however, the country's then army chief, General Abdel Fattah el-Sisi deposed Morsi and his Islamist government in a bloodless coup d'état in July 2013. In addition to an immediate suspension of the 2012 constitution, the FJP was banned and dissolved in 2014. The whole episode was actually a swing of the pendulum

---

[419] Cook, pp. 65, 257.

[420] William B. Quandt, *Camp David: Peacemaking and Politics* (Washington, D.C.: The Brookings Institution, 1986), pp. 176–177.

[421] Jason Brownlee, *Democracy Prevention: The Politics of the U.S.-Egyptian Alliance* (New York: Cambridge University Press, 2012).

---

to the old system previously run by presidents Anwar Sadat and Hosni Mubarak. Egypt under el-Sisi swiftly abandoned its Morsi-style approach toward the outside world, partly because the whole Egyptian political and economic establishment had been badly addicted to the privileges and perks which it had received over years through close cooperation with the United States and its Middle Eastern allies. Moreover, the el-Sisi-dominated government soon realized that Egypt's regional and international freedom had long been constrained by a litany of limitations, and it was in its best interest to simply remain faithful to the US-led order in the region.

Meanwhile, el-Sisi did not discard in total Egypt's recent orientation toward the East. His government needed to reappraise the looking-East approach by giving prominence to its economic and commercial objectives. Morsi's looking-East drive was going to be more inclusive encompassing almost all politico-strategic, military, economic, and cultural components.[422] But under el-Sisi, economic and trade issues were to trump ideological and geopolitical matters in Egypt's relationship with Asian countries. In this sense, el-Sisi differed from the old system which he rushed to revive after toppling the Morsi government.[423] Under Sadat and particularly Mubarak, Egypt's connections to Asia were mostly about politico-ideological as well as military interactions. But el-Sisi prioritized trade and commercial incentives, because his country's deteriorating economic circumstances could be alleviated considerably by attracting more rich and resourceful Asian companies and investors into Egypt.[424] In order to achieve this critical task, non-economic factors were expected to smooth the way, as usual.

Mutually intended: Capitalizing on the political springboard

Without making a serious attempt to play the West and the East off each other, Egypt has historically strived to benefit from its calculated relationship with both Western and Eastern powers. When Egypt was lured into a strategic alliance with the West in the late 1970s, for instance, Cairo still did its best to maintain a semblance of friendly relations with the Soviet Union. In the same way, when disagreements over Egypt's corruption and human rights records led to a dangerous deterioration in relations between the Obama administration and Cairo, the Egyptian government did not swiftly

---

[422] "Egypt Turns Quietly to Asia," *Middle East Institute*, February 25, 2013.
[423] "Egypt's Morsi Firms China Ties," *The Wall Street Journal*, August 29, 2012.
[424] "Chinese Firms Brave Uncertainty in Egypt to Gain a Foothold in the Middle East," *The New York Times*, August 29, 2012; and "Egypt Looking more Towards China for Trade, Development," *CCTV*, December 23, 2014.

turn its back on the West by clasping to the East's bosom.[425] Of course, Egypt approached a number of non-Western powers, Russia in particular, and the move ultimately resulted in signing a "strategic partnership" treaty between Cairo and Moscow in October 2018, but the Egyptian tactic was largely to buy time before the Middle Eastern country could regain its important position in Washington and be recompensed by the Trump administration.[426]

Egypt's looking-East orientation turned out to be no exception to that general pattern. Excluding the Morsi presidency, the Egyptian looking-East was not intended to compromise Cairo's beneficial connections to the West. Likewise, Egypt in the East was very cautious not to give this impression that it was prioritizing one major power over another. Cairo succeeded in elevating its old ties with China to the level of "comprehensive strategic partnership" in 2014, but such an advance in bilateral relationship with the rising Asian power did not really imply that Beijing could soon take the political place of Moscow for Egypt regardless of the fact that the Chinese had emerged, as anticipated, as the largest economic partner of Cairo since 2012.[427] Egypt demonstrated a similar behavior vis-à-vis India as well. The two nations were once at the forefront of Eastern struggle against Western colonialism, and such a consequential companionship was to be further enhanced through a close cooperation between Cairo and New Delhi within the NAM. But the two countries moved beyond the memories of those days, as pragmatism—and not the erstwhile idealism—was the mainspring behind their current attitudes toward the international system.[428]

By comparison, Egypt's looking-East approach toward other important Asian players happened to be fair and square without numerous political intricacies. Egypt's improved relationship with Japan and South Korea since 2016 onward was to ultimately translate into certain commercial advantages for Cairo, though both Tokyo and Seoul still needed an understanding and cooperation of the Egyptian government with regard to the North Korean nuclear controversy and the implementation of international sanctions levied against Pyongyang.[429] In September 2016, moreover, Egypt acceded to

---

[425] "Egypt Looks East," *Al Ahram Weekly*, September 14, 2017; and "Egypt Looks East to Expand Its Diverse Foreign Relations," *Arab News*, October 25, 2018.

[426] "Trump Praises Egypt's Sissi despite Concerns about Human Rights," *Voice of America*, April 9, 2019.

[427] "China, Egypt Elevate Bilateral Ties to Comprehensive Strategic Partnership," *CCTV*, December 24, 2014; and "Egypt Loves China's Deep Pockets," *Foreign Policy*, August 28, 2018.

[428] Theodor Tudoroiu, "Assessing Middle Eastern Trajectories: Egypt after Mubarak," *Contemporary Politics*, Vol. 17, No. 4 (2011), pp. 373–391.

[429] El-Sisi made an official visit to both Japan and South Korea in early 2016. Besides upgrading Cairo's relations with Seoul to the level of "comprehensive strategic part-

the Treaty of Amity and Cooperation in Southeast Asia (TAC), smoothing the way for better connections with the ASEAN members many of which were already keen to foster closer ties with the Arab country. In fact, Egypt, along with Morocco, became the first North African nations to accede the TAC which already had 35 signatories from around the world.[430] A confluence of such developments in Egypt's relationship with Asian countries, therefore, signified that the Egyptian government was in favor of a balanced and future-oriented approach toward the East without jeopardizing its fundamental interests in the West.[431]

For its part, Egypt enjoyed certain advantages which could significantly boost its looking-East progress with many Asian players. As a leading Arab country, Egypt had long been a major target of various important policies and strategies pursued by Eastern powers in the Middle East. This was actually a crucial factor long before Egypt upped the ante by joining a politically calculated and economically rewarding alliance with the West in the late 1970s. Once Egypt got involved in the Camp David Accords and, in sharp contrast to most of its Arab counterparts, recognized Israel as a sovereign state in the Middle East, moreover, its potential contribution to peace and stability in the region persuaded many Asian countries to hold the Arab country in high regard.[432] Since some of those Eastern stakeholders were either unable or unwilling to contribute anything substantial to the pivotal region's peace and stability, they wanted to be acknowledged as responsible beneficiaries simply by appreciating the role played by the Egyptians.[433]

In addition to its influential political role in the Middle East, Egypt also mattered as a geopolitical issue for many Eastern nations. By dint of its important location, Egypt could serve the East literally as a gateway to the broader African continent far beyond the Middle East. As time went by, almost all the growing Asian powers carved out ambitious plans to expand their politico-economic footprint in Africa.[434] Egypt could facilitate those

nership," he also became the first Arab and second African leader to deliver a speech at Japan's parliament, known as the Diet.

[430] "Egypt Eyes Closer Ties with ASEAN," *The Myanmar Times*, May 15, 2017.

[431] Robert D. Springborg, "Egypt's Future: Yet another Turkish Model?" *The International Spectator*, Vol. 49, No. 1 (2014), pp. 1–6.

[432] "Shoukry Receives Chinese Envoy for Middle East," *Daily News Egypt*, October 14, 2014; and "Japan, Egypt to Work to Bring Stability to Middle East," *The Mainichi*, October 6, 2018.

[433] "China Supports Egypt to Promote Stability, Economic Growth: FM," *Xinhua*, August 4, 2014; and "Chinese Vice President Meets AL Chief, Egyptian FM," *Global Times*, July 10, 2018.

[434] Daniel Large, "Beyond 'Dragon in the Bush': The Study of China–Africa Relations," *African Affairs*, Vol. 107, No. 426 (2008), pp. 45–61; Howard W. French, *China's Second Continent: How a Million Migrants Are Building a New Empire in Africa* (New York: Alfred A.

crucial objectives by linking Asian countries with Africa. Part of this significance stemmed from the Suez Canal, which made the Egyptian location so highly advantageous. Thus, it is no coincidence that the Suez Canal was placed at the heart of China's maritime Silk Road. Beijing became the biggest foreign investor in the strategic waterway. The Chinese needed to get Egypt deeply involved in that mega plan in order to carry out their projects in the region.[435]

Soft and subterranean: Gearing toward larger arms deals

Egypt's foreign and security policies toward the outside world, including the looking-East orientation, has long been greatly influenced by the military. In fact, since the 1952 putsch which replaced the Egyptian monarchy with a republic, the military has played an indispensable role in almost every aspect of the country's domestic and foreign affairs. On top of that, the military has often portrayed itself as the country's ultimate savior by promising to bring stability and prosperity to the Egyptian society.[436] The positive reputation of the Egyptian military's capacity and function was instrumental in rallying a great percentage of the disenchanted citizenry behind the armed forces in the run-up to the overthrow of the Morsi government by the el-Sisi-led putschist generals in July 2013.[437] It was largely for the same reason that el-Sisi was able to quickly establish its power and influence among many ordinary and middle-class Egyptians. He had enough charm and charisma to be reelected for a second term in the presidential elections held in March 2018.[438]

As an implication of the military's overarching status and role, therefore, Egypt has become a major importer of armaments in the world. Based on some estimates, under el-Sisi Egypt's demand for foreign munitions expanded exponentially and turned the Arab country into the world's third biggest purchaser of arms behind Saudi Arabia and India. Of course, reports

---

Knopf, 2014); and "Could Egypt Become the Next Member of the BRICS?" *Global Times*, September 14, 2017.

[435] "Xi Meets Egyptian President," *Xinhua*, April 25, 2019; and "Sisi Sees Great Promise in China–Egypt Partnerships," *Al-Monitor*, May 1, 2019.

[436] Joshua Stacher, *Adaptable Autocrats: Regime Power in Egypt and Syria* (Stanford, CA: Stanford University Press, 2012), pp. 60, 62.

[437] Cook, *False Dawn*, p. 241.

[438] Many opposition forces inside and outside the country as well as different human rights groups, however, dismissed the whole election process as "sham" and "farcical" because they accused the Egyptian authorities of "trampling over even the minimum requirements for free and fair elections." For more details, see: "Failure to Launch: Egypt Opposition Hits Roadblock on Path to Presidency," *Reuters*, January 21, 2018; and "Egypt: Planned Presidential Vote Neither Free Nor Fair," *Human Rights Watch*, February 13, 2018.

have published different data and statistics on Egypt's military deals, but it is generally gauged that over the past decade the Middle Eastern country has signed arms transfer agreements worth billions of dollars, a great part of which was bankrolled by loans requested from global institutions such as the International Monetary Fund (IMF), and lending and financial credits asked from some well-to-do Arab countries like Saudi Arabia and the United Arab Emirates. The major exporters of conventional and advanced weaponry to Egypt have been the United States, Western European countries and Russia.[439]

Despite the crucial role of the West as the principal purveyor of Egypt's arms imports, the East is becoming more and more attractive for Egyptian military orders. Russia has certainly been a major supplier of arms to Egypt for decades, and history has proved that whenever Cairo encountered serious impediments to buying military equipment from the West, it swiftly turned to Russians for arms assistance.[440] Besides Russia, a number of Asian countries are now striving to build their share of Egypt's arms market, and the new Egyptian looking-East is very conducive to such a trend.[441] It is no coincidence that Egypt has become the second biggest buyer of Chinese drones after Pakistan, purchasing some 23 percent of all drones China exports. Since 2016, moreover, Egyptian and Chinese officials have reportedly held several meetings about promoting their military and defense cooperation, but they are yet to agree on any substantial arms transfers from Beijing to Cairo.[442] The Egyptian government has obviously been under mounting pressure from the United States and some of its allies not to engage in larger volumes of military deals with China; Cairo would risk pressures similar to those it experienced over a North Korea-related incident a couple of years earlier.

In August 2016, Egyptian customs officials, acting on a tip from the United States, boarded the *Jie Shun*, a bulk freighter sailing through the Suez Canal under the Cambodian flag, carrying more than 30,000 PG-7 rocket-propelled grenades. The cargo, which was estimated to worth $23 million, had been actually purchased by some Egyptian businessmen on behalf of the Egyptian military; a tactic whereby the two countries had previously engaged in clandestine arms deals by taking advantage of private businesses

[439] Congressional Research Service, *Conventional Arms Transfers to Developing Nations, 2008–2015* (Washington, D.C.: Congressional Research Service, December 19, 2016), pp. 11–13.

[440] William J. Burns, *Economic Aid and American Policy toward Egypt, 1955–1981* (Albany, NY: State University of New York Press, 1985), p. 8; and "Egypt Signs $2bn Deal for 20 Russian Fighter Jets," *Middle East Monitor*, March 19, 2019.

[441] "Egypt Defence Expo Highlights Cairo's Diversified Military Strategy," *The National*, December 8, 2018.

[442] "China is Flooding the Middle East with Cheap Drones," *Foreign Policy In Focus*, February 18, 2019.

and front firms such as the North Korean Ocean Maritime Management Company (OMM).[443] That episode, which was reported by the *Washington Post* more than a year later, propelled the Trump administration to freeze or delay, albeit temporarily, millions of dollars of military and economic aids to Egypt.[444] Egypt and North Korea had a long history of military cooperation dating back to the 1970s when Pyongyang dispatched its military technicians and pilots to help Cairo in the Yom Kippur War of 1973, but the Americans were now demanding certain concrete actions by the Egyptian government in order to further punish Pyongyang over its "provocative" missile and nuclear programs.[445]

In order to save face and not to lose the advantages deriving from a good relationship with Washington, therefore, Egypt announced through its Defense Minister, Sidki Sobhi, who was on an official visit to Seoul in September 2017, that it had severed all military ties with North Korea.[446] But the Egyptian government simply did not confirm Sobhi's proclamation, and several Egyptian news outlets which posted his comments soon edited out the very statement he had made in Seoul.

Not only did the Egyptians refrain from rupturing their military relationship with North Korea as demanded by the United States, they moved to strengthen their level of military and defense cooperation with South Korea, though Washington probably had little, if any, reservation about such type of bilateral interactions involving Cairo and Seoul.[447] In fact, the two countries had started to negotiate over exporting South Korea's K-9 howitzers to Egypt sometime in 2010, but their talks had come to standstill largely due to the ensuing political tumults in Cairo which eventually led to the ascendency of el-Sisi. Sobhi had now been given the mandate by the Egyptian government to resume the negotiations with South Korea after a string of K-9 howitzers had been taken to Egypt for performance evaluation tests. In

---

[443] As a matter of fact, Egyptians and their counterparts from the communist regime of North Korea have been engaging each other in politico-diplomatic, military, and economic areas for more than four decades. Egypt is one of three Arab states (which include Syria and the Palestinian National Authority) that has a functioning embassy in Pyongyang, and it is also one of the five Arab countries (the other states include Algeria, Libya, Syria, and Kuwait) that hosts a North Korean embassy in its political capital.

[444] "A North Korean Ship was Seized off Egypt with a Huge Cache of Weapons Destined for a Surprising Buyer," *The Washington Post*, October 1, 2017; and "Why US Aid to Egypt is Never under Threat," *Al Jazeera*, October 3, 2017.

[445] Azad, *Koreans in the Persian Gulf*, p.38.

[446] "Yonhap Report: Egypt Cuts Military Ties with North Korea," *The Asahi Shimbun*, September 13, 2017.

[447] "Egypt Interested in Buying K-9 Howitzer," *Korea Times*, July 26, 2017; "Why is Egypt's Sisi Buying Arms from Kim Jong Un?" *Newsweek*, September 19, 2017; and "Government Considering Sending GSDF Personnel to Multinational Peacekeeping Force in Egypt," *The Japan Times*, September 17, 2018.

addition to the K-9 howitzer issue, Egypt and South Korea discussed several ways of expanding their military and defense relations, including the feasibility of joint-venture programs between their industries.[448]

Economy in the limelight: Expecting a "miracle on the ground"

Despite its huge potential, Egypt has hardly been a successful model in terms of transforming the economic circumstances of its average citizens. In the early 1960s, for instance, Egypt and South Korea had roughly the same income per capita, but today the small East Asian country's income per capita is more than 12 times as high as Egypt's.[449] Of course, successive Egyptian governments carved out their own economic and development plans, dating back to the mid-1970s when Anwar Sadat's policy of al-infitah (economic opening) aimed to increase the role of private sector by a gradual replacement of the state-led development strategy.[450] The agenda of economic reform gained momentum under Mubarak in the early 1990s, when the government pushed for more liberalization and privatization of state-owned enterprises. Since 2004, Mubarak accelerated the pace of his economic transformation by implementing neoliberal measures. This style of economic prescription proved to be bitter medicine for a society like Egypt, triggering more public demonstrations and strikes, which eventually levered the Mubarak regime out of power in early 2011.[451]

Egypt's worsening economic upheavals and its simmering financial predicament played a critical role in pushing it to look East in the post-Mubarak era.[452] As a nation of more than 100 million people, the 14th most populous country in the world and the most populous one in the entire Middle East and North African region, Egypt was already importing about 60–70 percent of its food, while its battered economy constantly had to bear

---

[448] "S. Korea, Egypt Vow Ties on N. Korea, Defense Industry," *Korea Times*, September 11, 2017; and "Egyptian Navy to Receive South Korean Vessel," *Egypt Independent*, September 19, 2017.

[449] Based on the IMF's 2018 data, the GDP per capita of South Korea and Egypt is $31,346 and $2,573, making them the 12th and 43th largest economies in the world, respectively.

[450] Matthew Gray, "Economic Reform, Privatization and Tourism in Egypt," *Middle Eastern Studies*, Vol. 34, No. 2 (1998), pp. 91–112; and Bruce K. Rutherford, *Egypt after Mubarak: Liberalism, Islam, and Democracy in the Arab World* (Princeton and Oxford: Princeton University Press, 2013), p. ix.

[451] Joel Beinin, "Workers' Protest in Egypt: Neo-liberalism and Class Struggle in 21st Century," *Social Movement Studies*, Vol. 8, No. 4 (2009), pp. 449–454; and Lloyd C. Gardner, *The Road to Tahrir Square: Egypt and the United States from the Rise of Nasser to the Fall of Mubarak* (New York: The New Press, 2011).

[452] "Egypt Looks East after Arab Spring," *Japan International Cooperation Agency*, March 19, 2013; and "Egypt's Shifting Foreign Policy Priorities," *The Cairo Review of Global Affairs*, spring 2018.

with considerably large trade deficits as well. Under such dire economic circumstances, what Egypt could usually expect from the West was a reluctant offer of expensive loans and an unyielding package of neoliberal shock-therapy.[453] Although the el-Sisi government still had to make a hard deal to secure a $12 billion loan from the IMF in exchange for carrying out some far-reaching economic reforms, the Egyptian looking-East orientation was developed in hopes of finding some less painful and more fruitful economic assistance from Asian countries. Conventionally, offers of financial aid and economic assistance from the East were free of any political strings, but the Egyptian government now wanted a new chapter in bilateral relationships with Asian countries to bring about more symbiotic economic connections and longer benefits for a larger number of its citizens.[454]

Among all Asian countries, China appeared to be the most appealing with regard to a potential fulfillment of Egypt's new looking-East objectives. It had become Cairo's largest trading partner since 2012, and Xi Jinping's attachment to the Belt and Road Initiative, and especially the maritime Silk Road, dovetailed neatly enough with what the Egyptian government desired from its new approach toward Asia.[455] Offering loans and direct involvement, the Chinese were more resourceful and willing to participate in a broad range of state-led massive projects particularly the New Administrative Capital and its Central Business District which the el-Sisi government initiated.[456] More than 1,500 Chinese companies ended up operating in a whole host of economic sectors in Egypt, including manufacturing, telecommunications, and infrastructure development projects. From helping Egypt to carry out electric power transformation to participating in the country's service sector, the Chinese inevitably enhanced their share of market pene-

[453] Loans and any other type of financial help from other regions and countries were obviously not going to be offered to Egypt on a silver platter either. As a case point, Egypt under el-Sisi apparently needed to sign a maritime dispute agreement with Saudi Arabia in order to receive some generous Saudi loans and credits. The deal, which was ultimately approved by the Egyptian parliament in June 2017 despite huge public outcry, required Cairo to cede officially to Saudi Arabia sovereignty of two Red Sea islands, Tiran and Sanafir.

[454] Paul Rivlin, "Egypt's Economic Woes and the Chinese Model," *Middle Eastern Studies*, Vol. 46, No. 6 (2010), pp. 957–964.

[455] "Aiji zhuhua dashi: 'Yidai yilu' qihe aiji 'xiang dong kan'" [Egypt's Ambassador to China: 'One Belt, One Road' Dovetails with Egypt's 'Looking-East'], *Renmin*, February 24, 2016; "Egypt Loves China's Deep Pockets," *Foreign Policy*, August 28, 2018; and "Egypt Looks East to Expand Its Diverse Foreign Relations," *Arab News*, October 25, 2018.

[456] "China Supports Egypt to Promote Stability, Economic Growth: FM," *Xinhua*, August 4, 2014; and "China–Egypt Ties to Grow under Partnership," *Global Times*, August 5, 2018.

tration and thereby widened the already growing trade deficit between the two nations in favor of Beijing.[457]

Despite the fact that probably only China could play a determining role in materializing what some Egyptian officials anticipated to be a "miracle on the ground," other major economic powers such as Japan, South Korea and India were in a position to lend a helping hand as well. In particular, India was considered to be a major destination for Egyptian exports in the long run, making it vital for Cairo to foster better politico-economic connections to New Delhi. Egypt also tried to gain Indian support for joining the BRICS bloc, though such a quest was futile given the poor performance of the Egyptian economy and a lack of enough sympathy from most BRICS members.[458] Still, India, like other major commercial countries of the East, was expected to play an instrumental role in the long-term in developing the special economic zone of the Suez Canal, turning it from a mere maritime route with limited revenues into a financially rewarding logistical and service hub for international commerce. More than 60 percent of Chinese exports to Europe were passing through the Suez Canal, and the critical passageway could easily perform a similar function for a rising export power like India.[459]

Meanwhile, Egypt's new looking-East push was not only about working with the most powerful and thriving Asian economies. As the case of Telecom Orascom in North Korea had already demonstrated, the Egyptians were prepared to engage less developed and resource-rich parts of Asia.[460] ASEAN countries like Vietnam and Indonesia were particularly alluring no matter if they were unable for now to contribute to development projects in the Suez Canal. The post-Mubarak Egypt had to compete even with its small regional rivals in North Africa, such as Tunisia and Morocco, so forging closer economic ties with ASEAN countries could indeed prove that Egypt offered considerable prospects for international trade and business. After all, the large population of Egypt could make it a lucrative consumer market

---

[457] Although Egypt strived to export to China even its stray dogs and live donkeys, Cairo could still hardly make a serious dent in the large edifice of its trade imbalance vis-à-vis Beijing.

[458] "Could Egypt Become the Next Member of the BRICS?" *Global Times*, September 14, 2017.

[459] "India–Egypt Bilateral Trade Rises by 33%," *Economic Times*, October 13, 2012; and "Egypt President to Visit India Next Month," *Times of India*, February 7, 2013.

[460] In 2008, Orascom, an Egyptian telecommunications firm, in cooperation with the communist regime of Pyongyang, established Koryolink, North Korea's only mobile phone network. As part of the profitable deal, Orascom secured a 75 percent stake, and the other 25 percent owned by North Korea. Despite the reportedly ensuing problems between the Egyptian company and its host country, the business partnership was another illustration of long-term overt and covert dealings between Cairo and Pyongyang. For more details, see: "Egyptian Tycoon Stumbles in North Korea," *The Wall Street Journal*, January 1, 2016; and "'Egypt's Orascom Stops Service in N. Korea'," *Korea Times*, December 19, 2017.

for cheap goods produced by ambitious ASEAN members like Vietnam. By attracting more foreign investors from the ASEAN region, therefore, Egypt could promote itself as a rewarding destination for more affluent and accomplished businesses from other parts of Asia.[461]

Untrammeled: Bringing cultural magnetism into play

Apart from geopolitics and natural endowments, the cultural attributes of Egypt could be exploited to grease the wheels of its new looking-East drive. In fact, the claim of some scholars that the genesis of Chinese civilization can be traced back to ancient Egypt could actually persuade crowds of Asians to involve themselves in the Middle Eastern country far beyond tokenistic cultural exchanges.[462] Moreover, Egypt has long been a top choice of Asians seeking to learn the Arabic language and delve into Islamic studies. As a case in point, one of the early ambassadors of Taiwan to Saudi Arabia had an education from Egypt's Cairo University.[463] In the same way, today Cairo is home to thousands of Chinese Uighurs who move to Egypt to learn Arabic, engage in Islamic studies, and experience life in a thoroughly Muslim society.[464] A good number of well-known Asian politicians, managers, and scholars have studied in Egypt and presently play an instrumental role in promoting closer tie-in between their country and Egyptians in different fields.

Currently, however, tourism is the most prominent aspect of Egypt's cultural interactions with other parts of the world, including many Asian countries. Tourism is one of the main pillars of Egyptian economy, contributing some $30 billion to its GNP and supporting roughly 2.5 million jobs or 9.5 percent of the total employment in Egypt. This service sector is also the fastest growing industry in North Africa and its share of Egypt's total exports is more than 27 percent.[465]

The nationality of tourists and foreign visitors to the Middle Eastern country is undergoing significant changes. For many years, European and Arab tourists comprised the majority of the people who visited Egypt for

[461]"Egypt Looks East," *Al Ahram Weekly*, September 14, 2017.

[462]"Lessons for Egypt from East Asia," *Ahram Online*, September 13, 2015; "Does Chinese Civilization Come From Ancient Egypt?" *Foreign Policy*, September 2, 2016; and "Chinese Culture Day Embraces Egyptian civilization," *Global Times*, October 9, 2018.

[463]Azad, *Koreans in Iran*, p. 15.

[464]"Egypt Rounds up Uyghur Muslims at Behest of China," *Middle East Eye*, July 6, 2017; and "Egypt Aided Chinese Officials to Detain and 'Interrogate' Uighur Students," *Middle East Eye*, August 18, 2019.

[465]"Travel, tourism contribute to Egypt's GDP by 11.9%," *Egypt Today*, March 19, 2019; and "Egyptian Tourism Sees 50% Revenue Increase in 2018," *Egypt Independent*, April 8, 2019.

leisure and recreational purposes.[466] The tourism industry in Egypt still hinges on this group of foreign travelers for the bulk of its revenues, but Asian tourists are becoming an increasingly important contributor of foreign exchange to Egypt. Swarms of Chinese, Japanese, Korean, and Indian sight-seers and excursionists now visit every nook and cranny of Egypt, establishing themselves more and more among the high-spending foreign travelers in the country.[467]

Egypt has recognized the growing role of Asian travelers as one of the most up-and-coming markets for Egyptian tourism in the long run. After the political tumult in the post-Mubarak era, which took a heavy toll on the Egyptian tourism industry for a couple of years, the el-Sisi government paid particular attention to diversifying the country's tourist markets by promoting the industry in Asian countries.[468] Tourism in Egypt is certainly on the rebound after several years of grappling with an array of political and economic afflictions, but the Egyptian government is now even more determined to find creative ways to encourage a greater number of well-heeled Asians to include Egypt in their foreign travel itinerary — and to spend money while they are there. In addition to signing agreements with Asian countries to establish several new air routes with Egyptian cities, the government has attempted to convince Asian investors to pour their hard cash and technical know-how into upgrading tourism infrastructures in major recreational hot spots across Egypt.[469]

Conclusion

Deep down, Egypt is a veteran while at the same time an underachieving latecomer to the concept of looking-East. Egypt launched an Eastward-facing component in its foreign policy zeitgeist earlier than its peers, establishing early connections with several Asian countries from the 1950s onward. Most of these initial interactions between Egypt and its close counterparts in the East, however, revolved around ideological, political, and military matters. All these areas of bilateral relationships could certainly warrant fruitful

---

[466] Brian Fagan, *The Rape of the Nile: Tomb Robbers, Tourists, and Archaeologists in Egypt*, third edition (Boulder, CO: Westview Press, 2004); and Anthony Sattin, *Lifting the Veil: Two Centuries of Travellers, Traders and Tourists in Egypt* (London and New York: I.B. Tauris, 2011).

[467] "Court Denies Egyptian Refugee Status for Homosexuality," *Korea Times*, July 12, 2017; "Korean Tourist Dies While Snorkeling in Egypt," *Korea Times*, October 10, 2018; and "126,000 Indian tourists visited Egypt in 2018: official," *Egypt Independent*, March 18, 2019.

[468] "Egypt Eyes Asian Tourists," *Al-Monitor*, March 1, 2019.

[469] "Korean Investment in Egypt Unswayed by Arab Spring," May 31, *Korea Times*, 2015; "Egypt's Nile River Hosts Dragon Boat Festival to Celebrate Chinese New Year," *Global Times*, February 25, 2019; and "China Promising Market for Egypt's Tourism: Minister," *Xinhua*, April 4, 2019.

economic and financial ties between Egypt and Asian countries in the long term, too. But the problem was that succeeding governments in Egypt made little, if any, strategic calculations with regard to the huge economic promise represented by a swiftly rising East. Moreover, Cairo had gradually come to feel comfortable in the cocoon of the security alliance it made with the United States in the late 1970s. As a consequence, Egypt became addicted to the post-Camp David system, prioritizing politico-financial rewards coming from continuous close cooperation between Cairo and its partners in the region and beyond.

By the time the Egyptian government embarked upon a looking-East orientation in earnest in the post-Mubarak era, therefore, the country had already missed significant opportunities without any real tangible results from its relationship with Asia spanning more than six and half decades. Only the new economic realities in Egypt, coupled with the bright prospect of a rising East, convinced the government in Cairo to take better care of its relations with Asian countries. Excepting the Morsi presidency, the new looking-East drive in Egypt, however, strived to distance itself from the erstwhile politico-ideological imperatives in favor of achieving immediate economic and financial benefits by cultivating larger exchanges with Asian nations. Mutually beneficial bilateral connections survived in other areas, including the political and military realms, but it was the economic parameter which now needed to be strengthened.

To sum up, the prospect of Egypt's looking-East approach will largely depend on how much the government in Cairo can persuade the resourceful and rising Asian powers to invest more in the Middle Eastern country. Egypt certainly has unique geopolitical, demographic, and cultural advantages which can be exploited in order to win over well-to-do Asian nations to share their capital and technological capabilities with the Egyptians.

This is obviously a challenging exercise, but a more daunting task is how to achieve a national consensus in Egypt with regard to applying itself seriously to carrying out a large-scale program of economic growth and development. For a country like Egypt, coming up with such an ambitious national agenda is long overdue. Only by following such a grand strategy can Egypt benefit sufficiently and deservedly from its huge potential in various areas. Sticking firmly to this mega plan of national rejuvenation would also elevate Egypt's attraction among Asian countries and smooth the way for higher levels of productive partnership in fields favorable to both sides.

Bibliography

Aarts, Paul. "Saudi Arabia Walks the Tightrope." *The International Spectator* 42, no. 4 (2007): 545–550.

Abadi, Jacob. *Israel's Quest for Recognition and Acceptance in Asia: Garrison State Diplomacy.* London: Frank Cass Publishers, 2004.

Adelman, Jonathan. *The Rise of Israel: A History of a Revolutionary State.* Abingdon and New York: Routledge, 2008.

Andres, Richard. "The Afghan Model in Northern Iraq." *Journal of Strategic Studies* 29, no. 3 (2006): 395–422.

Azad, Shirzad. "Japan's Gulf Policy and Response to the Iraq War." *The Middle East Review of International Affairs* 12, no. 2 (June 2008): 52–64.

_____. "Iran and the Two Koreas: A Peculiar Pattern of Foreign Policy." *The Journal of East Asian Affairs* 26, no. 2 (fall/winter 2012): 163–192.

_____. *Koreans in the Persian Gulf: Policies and International Relations.* Abingdon and New York: Routledge, 2015.

_____. "Principalism Engages Pragmatism: Iran's Relations with East Asia under Ahmadinejad." *Asian Politics & Policy* 7, no. 4 (October 2015): 555–573.

_____. *Iran and China: A New Approach to Their Bilateral Relations.* Lanham, MD: Lexington Books, 2017.

_____. *Koreans in Iran: Missiles, Markets and Myths.* New York: Algora Publishing, 2018.

_____. *East Asian Politico-Economic Ties with the Middle East: Newcomers, Trailblazers, and Unsung Stakeholders.* New York: Algora Publishing, 2019.

Baer, Robert. *Sleeping with the Devil: How Washington Sold Our Soul for Saudi Crude.* New York: Three Rivers Press, 2004.

Bard, Mitchell. *The Arab Lobby: The Invisible Alliance that Undermines America's Interests in the Middle East.* New York: HarperCollins Publishers, 2010.

Barkey, Henri J. "Turkey and the New Middle East: A Geopolitical Exploration." In *Reluctant Neighbor: Turkey's Role in the Middle East,* edited by Henri J. Barkey. Washington D.C.: The United States Institute of Peace Press, 1996.

Bartu, Friedemann. *The Ugly Japanese: Nippon's Economic Empire in Asia.* Singapore: Longman, 1992.

Beinin, Joel. "Workers' Protest in Egypt: Neo-liberalism and Class Struggle in 21st Century." *Social Movement Studies* 8, no. 4 (2009): 449–454.

Beyme, Klaus von. "Redefining European Security: The Role of German Foreign Policy." In *Redefining European Security,* edited by Carl C. Hodge. New York and London: Garland Publishing, 1999.

Bianchi, Robert R. *Guests of God: Pilgrimage and Politics in the Islamic World.* New York: Oxford University Press, 2004.

Bill, James A. *The Eagle and the Lion: The Tragedy of American–Iranian Relations.* New Haven and London: Yale University Press, 1988.

Billon, Philippe L. "Corruption, Reconstruction and Oil Governance in Iraq." *Third World Quarterly* 26, no. 4–5 (2005): 685–703.

Bing, Feng. *"Yidai yilu": Quanqiu fazhande zhongguo luoji* ["One Belt, One Road": The Chinese Logic for Global Development]. Beijing: Zhongguo minzhu fazhi chubanshe, 2015.

Blanchard, Christopher M., and Paul K. Kerr. *United Arab Emirates Nuclear Program and Proposed U.S. Nuclear Cooperation,* CRS Report for Congress, December 23, 2009. Washington, D.C.: Congressional Research Service, 2009.

Blarel, Nicolas. "Assessing US Influence over India–Israel Relations: A Difficult Equation to Balance?" *Strategic Analysis* 41, no. 4 (2017): 384–400.

Brownlee, Jason. *Democracy Prevention: The Politics of the U.S.-Egyptian Alliance.* New York: Cambridge University Press, 2012.

Bruinessen, Martin van. *Agha, Shaikh and State: The Social and Political Structures of Kurdistan.* London: Zed Books, 1992.

Brzoska, Michael. "Profiteering on the Iran–Iraq War." *Bulletin of the Atomic Scientists* (June 1987): 42–45.

Buren, Peter V. *We Meant Well: How I Helped Lose the Battle for the Hearts and Minds of the Iraqi People.* New York: Metropolitan Books, 2011.

Burns, William J. *Economic Aid and American Policy toward Egypt, 1955–1981*. Albany, NY: State University of New York Press, 1985.

Calabrese, John. "From Flyswatters to Silkworms: The Evolution of China's Role in West Asia." *Asian Survey* 30, no. 9 (September 1990): 862–876.

_____. *China's Changing Relations with the Middle East*. London and New York: Pinter Publishers, 1991.

Champion, Daryl. "The Kingdom of Saudi Arabia: Elements of Instability within Stability." *Middle East Review of International Affairs* 3, no. 4 (December 1999): 49–73.

Christie, Kenneth. "Globalisation, Religion and State Formation in the United Arab Emirates and Pakistan." *Totalitarian Movements and Political Religions* 11, no. 2 (2010): 203–212.

Codrai, Ronald. *The Seven Sheikhdoms: Life in the Trucial States before the Federation of the United Arab Emirates*. London: Stacey International, 1990.

Cohen, Goel. *Technology Transfer: Strategic Management in Developing Countries*. London: Sage Publications, 2004.

Congressional Research Service. *Conventional Arms Transfers to Developing Nations, 2008–2015*. Washington, D.C.: Congressional Research Service, December 19, 2016.

Cook, Steven A. *False Dawn: Protest, Democracy, and Violence in the New Middle East*. New York: Oxford University Press, 2017.

Cook, Steven A. *False Dawn: Protest, Democracy, and Violence in the New Middle East*. New York: Oxford University Press, 2017.

_____. *Ruling But Not Governing: The Military and Political Development in Egypt, Algeria, and Turkey*. Baltimore, MD: The Johns Hopkins University Press, 2007.

_____. *The Struggle for Egypt: From Nasser to Tahrir Square*. New York: Oxford University Press, 2012.

Cooper, Andrew S. *The Oil Kings: How the U.S., Iran, and Saudi Arabia Changed the Balance of Power in the Middle East*. New York: Simon & Schuster Paperbacks, 2011.

Cooper, Peter. *Opportunity Dubai: Making a Fortune in the Middle East*. Hampshire, UK: Harriman House LTD, 2008.

Cordesman, Anthony H. *The Iran–Iraq War and Western Security, 1984–1987: Strategic Implications and Policy Options*. London: Jane's Publishing, 1987.

Cronin, Patrick M., ed. *Double Trouble: Iran and North Korea as Challenges to International Security*. Westport, CT: Praeger Security International, 2008.

Crooke, Alastair. "You Can't Understand ISIS If You Don't Know the History of Wahhabism in Saudi Arabia." *New Perspectives Quarterly* 32, no. 1 (2015): 56–70.

Davidson, Christopher M. "Dubai and the United Arab Emirates: Security Threats." *British Journal of Middle Eastern Studies* 36, no. 3 (2009): 431–447.

_____. *Abu Dhabi: Oil and Beyond*. London: Hurst & Company, 2009.

_____. *After the Sheikhs: The Coming Collapse of the Gulf Monarchies*. New York: Oxford University Press, 2013.

Davutoğlu, Ahmet. "Zero Problems in a New Era: Realpolitik is No Answer to the Challenges Posed by the Arab Spring." *Foreign Policy*, March 21, 2013.

Dore, Ronald. "Japan in the Coming Century: Looking East or West?" In *Japan's Role in International Politics since World War II*, edited by Edward R. Beauchamp. New York and London: Garland Publishing, 1998.

Early, Bryan R. *Busted Sanctions: Explaining Why Economic Sanctions Fail*. Stanford, CA: Stanford University Press, 2015.

Eberling, George. *Chinese Energy Futures and Their Implications for the United States*. Lanham, MD: Lexington Books, 2011.

Egan, Daniel. "Globalization and the Invasion of Iraq: State Power and the Enforcement of Neoliberalism." *Sociological Focus* 40, no. 1 (2007): 98–111.

Eisenstadt, Michael. "Chinese Military Assistance to Iran: An Overview." In *Consequences of China's Military Sales to Iran: Hearing Before the Committee on International Relations, House of Representatives*, edited by Benjamin A. Gilman. One Hundred Fourth Congress, Second Session, September 12, 1996. Washington, D.C.: U.S. Government Printing Office, 1996.

Emerson, Steven. *The American House of Saud: The Secret Petrodollar Connection*. New York: Franklin Watts, 1985.

Evron, Yoram. "Between Beijing and Washington: Israel's Technology Transfers to China." *Journal of East Asian Studies* 13, no. 3 (2013): 503–528.

Fagan, Brian. *The Rape of the Nile: Tomb Robbers, Tourists, and Archaeologists in Egypt*, third edition. Boulder, CO: Westview Press, 2004.

Fallows, James. *Looking at the Sun: The Rise of the New East Asian Economic and Political System*. New York: Vintage Books, 1995.

Findley, Carter V. *The Turks in World History*. New York: Oxford University Press, 2005.

Flynn, Vince. *Consent to Kill: A Thriller*. New York: Atria Books, 2008.

Foley, Sean. "Re-Orientalizing the Gulf: The GCC and Southeast Asia." *Middle East Policy* 19, no. 4 (2012): 77–87.

Freedman, Lawrence. "Iraq, Liberal Wars and Illiberal Containment." *Survival* 48, no. 4 (2006): 51–66.

Freilich, Charles D. *Zion's Dilemmas: How Israel Makes National Security Policy.* Ithaca and London: Cornell University Press, 2012.

_____. "Can Israel Survive Without America?" *Survival* 59, no. 4 (2017): 135–150.

_____. *Israeli National Security: A New Strategy for an Era of Change.* New York: Oxford University Press, 2018.

French, Howard W. *China's Second Continent: How a Million Migrants Are Building a New Empire in Africa.* New York: Alfred A. Knopf, 2014.

Fuller, Graham E. *The New Turkish Republic: Turkey as a Pivotal State in the Muslim World.* Washington, D.C.: United States Institute of Peace Press, 2007.

Gardner, Lloyd C. *The Road to Tahrir Square: Egypt and the United States from the Rise of Nasser to the Fall of Mubarak.* New York: The New Press, 2011.

Garfinkle, Adam. *Politics and Society in Modern Israel: Myths and Realities,* second edition. New York and London: M.E. Sharpe, 2000.

Ghanim, David. *Iraq's Dysfunctional Democracy.* Santa Barbara, CA: Praeger, 2011.

Goldstein, Jonathan. "The Republic of China and Israel." In *China and Israel, 1948–1998: A Fifty Year Retrospective,* edited by Jonathan Goldstein. London: Praeger, 1999.

Gonzalez, Nathan. *Engaging Iran: The Rise of a Middle East Powerhouse and America's Strategic Choice.* Westport, CT: Praeger, 2007.

Graham, Robert. *Iran: The Illusion of Power.* New York: St. Martin's Press, 1978.

Gray, Matthew. "Economic Reform, Privatization and Tourism in Egypt." *Middle Eastern Studies* 34, no. 2 (1998): 91–112.

Gunter, Michael M. "Arab–Kurdish Relations and the Future of Iraq." *Third World Quarterly* 32, no. 9 (2011): 1623–1635.

_____. *The Kurds: A Modern History.* Princeton, NJ: Markus Wiener Publishers, 2016.

Hale, William M. *Turkish Politics and the Military.* London and New York: Routledge, 1994.

_____. *Turkish Foreign Policy, 1774–2000.* London: Frank Cass, 2000.

Hart, Parker T. *Saudi Arabia and the United States: Birth of a Security Partnership.* Bloomington, IN: Indiana University Press, 1998.

Herb, Michael. *The Wages of Oil: Parliaments and Economic Development in Kuwait and the UAE.* New York: Cornell University Press, 2014.

Hickey, Sean. *Confessions of an International Banker*. Bloomington, IN: Trafford Publishing, 2013.

Holt, Blaine D. "The Gold Standard: U.S.–Israel Military Relations." *American Foreign Policy Interests* 36, no. 2 (2014): 111–118.

Howard, Roger. "Why Israel Fears an Iranian Bomb." *The RUSI Journal* 150, no. 1 (2008): 65–69.

Howell, Leon, and Michael Morrow. *Asia, Oil Politics and the Energy Crisis: The Haves and the Have-nots*. New York: International Documentation, 1974.

Human Rights Watch. *"The Island of Happiness": Exploitation of Migrant Workers on Saadiyat Island, Abu Dhabi*. New York: Human Rights Watch, 2009.

International Institute for Strategic Studies (IISS). *The Military Balance 2019*. London: Routledge, 2019.

International Monetary Fund. *United Arab Emirates: Financial System Stability Assessment*. Washington, D.C.: International Monetary Fund, 2007.

_____. *United Arab Emirates: 2011 Article IV Consultation – Staff Report*. Washington, D.C.: International Monetary Fund, 2011.

Jacques, Martin. *When China Rules the World: The End of the Western World and the Birth of a New Global Order*, second edition. New York: Penguin Books, 2012.

Jin, Lu, and Zhang Liming. *Yilang: Dongxi fang wenming de huihe dian* [Iran: The Meeting Point of Eastern and Western Civilizations]. Hong Kong: Xiang-gang chengshi daxue chubanshe [City University of Hong Kong Press], 2011.

Jones, Bruce D. *Still Ours to Lead: America, Rising Powers, and the Tension between Rivalry and Restraint*. Washington, D.C.: Brookings Institution Press, 2014.

Katusa, Marin. *The Colder War: How the Global Energy Trade Slipped from America's Grasp*. Hoboken, NJ: John Wiley & Sons, 2015.

Katzman, Kenneth. *The Persian Gulf States: Post-War Issues*. New York: Novinka Books, 2004.

_____. *United Arab Emirates (UAE): Issues for U.S. Policy*. Washington, DC: Congressional Research Service Report for Congress, 2010.

Kinzer, Stephen. *Reset: Iran, Turkey, and America's Future*. New York: Times Books, 2010.

Krane, Jim. *Dubai: The Story of the World's Fastest City*. New York: St Martin's Press, 2009.

Kroeber, Arthur R. *China's Economy: What Everyone Needs to Know*. New York: Oxford University Press, 2016.

Kupchan, Charles A. *How Enemies Become Friends: The Sources of Stable Peace*. Princeton, NJ: Princeton University Press, 2010.

Lacey, Robert. *Inside the Kingdom: Kings, Clerics, Modernists, Terrorists and the Struggle for Saudi Arabia*. London: Arrow Books, 2009.

Lake, David A. *Hierarchy in International Relations*. Ithaca and London: Cornell University Press, 2009.

Lanteigne, Marc. *Chinese Foreign Policy: An Introduction*, third edition. Abingdon and New York: Routledge, 2016.

Large, Daniel. "Beyond 'Dragon in the Bush': The Study of China–Africa Relations." *African Affairs* 107, no. 426 (2008): 45–61.

Lawday, David. "Turkey Aims to be a Middle East Japan." *U.S. News & World Report* 111, no. 5 (July 29, 1991): 36.

Limbert, John W. *Iran: At War with History*. Boulder, CO: Westview Press, 1987.

Lippman, Thomas W. *Saudi Arabia on the Edge: The Uncertain Future of an American Ally*. Washington, D.C.: Potomac Books, 2012.

Looney, Robert E. "Saudi Arabian Budgetary Dilemmas." *Middle Eastern Studies* 26, no. 1 (1990): 76–87.

_____. "The IMF's Return to Iraq." *Challenge* 49, no. 3 (2006): 26–47.

Lorentz, John H. *The A to Z of Iran*. Lanham, MD: Scarecrow Press, 2007.

Lowenberg, Anton D., and Timothy Mathews. "Why Iraq?" *Defence and Peace Economics* 19, no. 1 (2008): 1–20.

Luce, Edward. *The Retreat of Western Liberalism*. New York: Atlantic Monthly Press, 2017.

Mahler, Gregory S. *Politics and Government in Israel: The Maturation of a Modern State*. Lanham, MD: Rowman & Littlefield, 2011.

Marzano, Arturo. "The Loneliness of Israel. The Jewish State's Status in International Relations." *The International Spectator* 48, no. 2 (2013): 96–113.

Mason, Robert. *Foreign Policy in Iran and Saudi Arabia: Economics and Diplomacy in the Middle East*. London and New York: I.B. Tauris, 2015.

McDowall, David. *A Modern History of the Kurds*, third edition. London and New York: I.B. Tauris, 2004.

McNally, Robert. *Crude Volatility: The History and the Future of Boom-Bust Oil Prices*. New York: Columbia University Press, 2017.

Mearsheimer, John J., and Stephen M. Walt. "Is It Love or the Lobby? Explaining America's Special Relationship with Israel." *Security Studies* 18, no. 1 (2009): 58–78.

Medeiros, Evan S. *China's International Behavior: Activism, Opportunism, and Diversification.* Santa Monica, CA: Rand Corporation, 2009.

Miller, Nicholas L., and Tristan A. Volpe. "Abstinence or Tolerance: Managing Nuclear Ambitions in Saudi Arabia." *The Washington Quarterly* 41, no. 2 (2018): 27–46.

Miller, Rory. *Desert Kingdoms to Global Powers: The Rise of the Arab Gulf.* New Haven, CT: Yale University Press, 2016.

Millward, James A. *The Silk Road: A Very Short Introduction.* New York: Oxford University Press, 2013.

Morris, Chris. *The New Turkey: The Quiet Revolution on the Edge of Europe.* London: Granta Publications, 2005.

Morton, Michael Q. *Keepers of the Golden Shore: A History of the United Arab Emirates.* London: Reaktion Books Ltd, 2016.

Mowle, Thomas S. "Iraq's Militia Problem." *Survival* 48, no. 3 (2006): 41–58.

Murphy, John F. *The Evolving Dimensions of International Law: Hard Choices for the World Community.* New York: Cambridge University Press, 2010.

Murray, Williamson, and Kevin M. Woods. *The Iran–Iraq War: A Military and Strategic History.* Cambridge, UK: Cambridge University Press, 2014.

Nugent, Brian. *In Defence of Conspiracy Theories: With Examples from Irish and International History and Politics.* London: Oldcastle, 2008.

O'Reilly, Marc J. *Unexceptional: America's Empire in the Persian Gulf, 1941–2007.* Lanham, MD: Lexington Books, 2008.

Oren, Michael B. *Ally: My Journey across the American–Israeli Divide.* New York: Random House, 2015.

Ottaway, David B. *The King's Messenger: Prince Bandar Bin Sultan, and America's Tangled Relationship with Saudi Arabia.* New York: Walker & Company: 2008.

Pack, Howard. "Asian Successes VS. Middle Eastern Failures: The Role of Technology Transfer in Economic Development." *Issues in Science and Technology* 24, no. 3 (Spring 2008): 47–54.

Parasiliti, Andrew. "Leaving Iraq." *Survival* 54, no. 1 (2012): 127–133.

Park, Bill. "The Kurds and Post-Saddam Political Arrangements in Iraq." *The Adelphi Papers* 45, no. 374 (2005): 29–48.

_____. *Modern Turkey: People, State and Foreign Policy in a Globalized World.* Abingdon and New York: Routledge, 2012.

_____. "Populism and Islamism in Turkey." *Turkish Studies* 19, no. 2 (November 2017): 169–175.

Parker, Thomas. "China's Growing Interests in the Persian Gulf." *The Brown Journal of World Affairs* 7, no. 1 (2000): 235–243.

Partrick, Neil, ed. *Saudi Arabian Foreign Policy: Conflict and Cooperation*. London and New York: I.B. Tauris, 2016.

Penn, Michael. *Japan and the War on Terror: Military Force and Political Pressure in the US–Japanese Alliance*. London and New York: I.B. Tauris, 2014.

Perkins, Dwight H. *East Asian Development: Foundations and Strategies*. Cambridge, MA: Harvard University Press, 2013.

Petras, James F. *The Power of Israel in the United States*. Atlanta: Clarity Press, 2006.

Phillips, Christopher. *The Battle for Syria: International Rivalry in the New Middle East*. New Haven and London: Yale University Press, 2016.

Pieper, Moritz. *Hegemony and Resistance around the Iranian Nuclear Programme: Analysing Chinese, Russian and Turkish Foreign Policies*. Abingdon and New York: Routledge, 2017.

Pierce, Jonathan J. "Oil and the House of Saud: Analysis of Saudi Arabian Oil Policy." *Digest of Middle East Studies* 21, no. 1 (2012): 89–107.

Polk, William R. *Understanding Iran: Everything You Need to Know, from Persia to the Islamic Republic, from Cyrus to Ahmadinejad*. New York: Palgrave Macmillan, 2009.

Pollock, David. "Israel's National Unity: Solution or Stalemate?" In *The Middle East from the Iran-Contra Affair to the Intifada*, edited by Robert Owen Freedman. New York: Syracuse University Press, 1991.

Posner, Gerald. *Secrets of the Kingdom: The Inside Story of the Secret Saudi–U.S. Connection*. New York: Random House, 2005.

Quandt, William B. *Camp David: Peacemaking and Politics*. Washington, D.C.: The Brookings Institution, 1986.

Ram, Haggai. *Iranophobia: The Logic of an Israeli Obsession*. Stanford, CA: Stanford University Press, 2009.

Raw, Laurence. *Exploring Turkish Cultures: Essays, Interviews and Reviews*. Newcastle upon Tyne, UK: Cambridge Scholars Publishing, 2011.

Reddy, Allan C. *A Macro Perspective on Technology Transfer*. Westport, Connecticut and London: Quorum Books, 1996.

Riedel, Bruce. *Kings and Presidents: Saudi Arabia and the United States since FDR*. Washington, D.C.: Brookings Institution Press, 2017.

Rivlin, Paul. "Egypt's Economic Woes and the Chinese Model." *Middle Eastern Studies* 46, no. 6 (2010): 957–964.

Robins, Philip. *Suits and Uniforms: Turkish Foreign Policy since the Cold War*. London: C. Hurst & Co., 2003.

Rosenberg, David. *Israel's Technology Economy: Origins and Impact*. New York: Palgrave Macmillan, 2018.

Ross, Michael L. *The Oil Curse: How Petroleum Wealth Shapes the Development of Nations*. Princeton and Oxford: Princeton University Press, 2012.

Roy, Denny. *Return of the Dragon: Rising China and Regional Security*. New York: Columbia University Press, 2013.

Rubin, Jared. *Rulers, Religion, and Riches: Why the West Got Rich and the Middle East Did Not*. New York: Cambridge University Press, 2017.

Rutherford, Bruce K. *Egypt after Mubarak: Liberalism, Islam, and Democracy in the Arab World*. Princeton and Oxford: Princeton University Press, 2013.

Sattin, Anthony. *Lifting the Veil: Two Centuries of Travellers, Traders and Tourists in Egypt*. London and New York: I.B. Tauris, 2011.

Schilling, Christopher L. "The Problem of Romanticising Israel–Taiwan Relations." *Israel Affairs* 24, no. 3 (2018): 460–466.

_____. *Emotional State Theory: Friendship and Fear in Israeli Foreign Policy*. Lanham, MD: Lexington Books, 2018.

Schmitt, Gary J., ed. *Rise of the Revisionists: Russia, China, and Iran*. Washington, D.C.: American Enterprise Institute, 2018.

Schroeder, Christopher M. *Startup Rising: The Entrepreneurial Revolution Remaking the Middle East*. New York: Palgrave Macmillan, 2013.

Schwarz, Rolf, and Oliver Jütersonke. "Divisible Sovereignty and the Reconstruction of Iraq." *Third World Quarterly* 26, no. 4–5 (2005): 649–665.

Schweizer, Peter. *Clinton Cash: The Untold Story of How and Why Foreign Governments and Businesses Helped Make Bill and Hillary Rich*. New York: HarperCollins Books, 2015.

Segal, Adam. "Chinese Economic Statecraft and the Political Economy." In *China's Rise and the Balance of Influence in Asia*, edited by William W. Keller and Thomas G. Rawski. Pittsburgh, PA: University of Pittsburgh Press, 2007.

Serwer, Daniel. "Muddling Through in Iraq." *Survival* 55, no. 4 (2013): 35–40.

Sevilla, Henelito A. Jr., ed. *Philippine–Iran Relations: 50 Years and Beyond*. Quezon City, Philippines: Asian Center, University of the Philippines Diliman, 2017.

Shapiro, Robert J. *Futurecast: How Superpowers, Populations, and Globalization Will Change Your World by the Year 2020*. New York: ST. Martin's Griffin, 2008.

Shelley, Fred M. *The World's Population: An Encyclopedia of Critical Issues, Crises, and Ever-Growing Countries*. Santa Barbara, CA: ABC-CLIO, 2015.

Shichor, Yitzhak. "Israel's Military Transfers to China and Taiwan." *Survival* 40, no. 1 (1998): 68–91.

Shindler, Colin. *A History of Modern Israel*, second edition. New York: Cambridge University Press, 2013.

Simmons, Matthew R. *Twilight in the Desert: The Coming Saudi Oil Shock and the World Economy*. Hoboken, NJ: John Wiley & Sons, 2005.

Simons, Geoffrey. *Saudi Arabia: The Shape of a Client Feudalism*. London: Macmillan, 1998.

Slater, Robert. *Seizing Power: The Grab for Global Oil Wealth*. Hoboken, NJ: John Wiley & Sons, 2010.

Smith, Benjamin B. *Hard Times in the Lands of Plenty: Oil Politics in Iran and Indonesia*. Ithaca, NY: Cornell University Press, 2007.

Springborg, Robert D. "Egypt's Future: Yet another Turkish Model?" *The International Spectator* 49, no. 1 (2014): 1–6.

Stacher, Joshua. *Adaptable Autocrats: Regime Power in Egypt and Syria*. Stanford, CA: Stanford University Press, 2012.

Steers, Richard M. *Made in Korea: Chung Ju Yung and the Rise of Hyundai*. New York: Routledge, 1999.

Stein, Aaron. *Turkey's New Foreign Policy: Davutoglu, the AKP and the Pursuit of Regional Order*. London: Royal United Services Institute for Defence and Security Studies, 2014.

Stenslie, Stig. *Regime Stability in Saudi Arabia: The Challenge of Succession*. Abingdon and New York: Routledge, 2012.

_____. "The End of Elite Unity and the Stability of Saudi Arabia." *The Washington Quarterly* 41, no. 1 (2018): 61–82.

Stetter, Stephan. *The Middle East and Globalization: Encounters and Horizons*. New York: Palgrave Macmillan, 2012.

Stockholm International Peace Research. *SIPRI Yearbook 2011: Armaments, Disarmament and International Security*. New York: Oxford University Press, 2011.

Stokes, Martin. *The Republic of Love: Cultural Intimacy in Turkish Popular Music*. Chicago and London: The University of Chicago Press, 2010.

Stone, Peter. "The Rape of Mesopotamia: Behind the Looting of the Iraq Museum." *Public Archaeology* 8, no. 4 (2009): 378–381.

Stroilov, Pavel. *Behind the Desert Storm: A Secret Archive Stolen from the Kremlin that Sheds New Light on the Arab Revolutions in the Middle East.* Chicago, IL: Price World Publishing, 2011.

Tal, David, ed. *Israeli Identity: Between Orient and Occident.* Abingdon and New York: Routledge, 2013.

Tarock, Adam. *The Superpowers' Involvement in the Iran–Iraq War.* Commack, NY: Nova Science Publishers, 1998.

The Financial Times. *Financial Times Oil and Gas International Year Book.* London: Longman, 1983.

The World Bank. *Strengthening China's and India's Trade and Investment Ties to the Middle East and North Africa.* Washington, D.C.: The World Bank, 2009.

Thies, Cameron G. *The United States, Israel, and the Search for International Order: Socializing States.* Abingdon and New York: Routledge, 2013.

Tudoroiu, Theodor. "Assessing Middle Eastern Trajectories: Egypt after Mubarak." *Contemporary Politics* 17, no. 4 (2011): 373–391.

Tunsjø, Øystein. *Security and Profit in China's Energy Policy: Hedging against Risk.* New York: Columbia University Press, 2013.

Tyler, Patrick. *Fortress Israel: The Inside Story of the Military Elite Who Run the Country – and Why They Can't Make Peace.* New York: Farrar, Straus and Giroux, 2012.

Unger, Craig. *House of Bush, House of Saud: The Secret Relationship between the World's Two Most Powerful Dynasties.* New York: Scribner, 2004.

United States Government Accountability Office (USGAO). *Iran Sanctions: Impact Good or Bad?* New York: Nova Science Publishers, 2008.

_____. *Iran Sanctions: Complete and Timely Licensing Data Needed to Strengthen Enforcement of Export Restrictions,* Report to Congressional Requesters, March 2010. Washington, D.C.: GAO, 2010.

Vitalis, Robert. *America's Kingdom: Mythmaking on the Saudi Oil Frontier.* Stanford, CA: Stanford University Press, 2007.

Walt, Stephen M. *The Hell of Good Intentions: America's Foreign Policy Elite and the Decline of U.S. Primacy.* New York: Farrar, Straus and Giroux, 2018.

Walzer, Michael. *A Foreign Policy for the Left.* New Haven and London: Yale University Press, 2018.

Weller, Marc. *Iraq and the Use of Force in International Law.* New York: Oxford University Press, 2010.

Wenar, Leif. *Blood Oil: Tyrants, Violence, and the Rules that Run the World.* New York: Oxford University Press, 2016.

Wilde, Felix. *Worldwide Development of Nuclear Energy: Strategic Deployment of German Consultancies in the Arabian Market.* Hamburg: Diplomica Verlag GmbH, 2011.

Williams, Phil. "Organized Crime and Corruption in Iraq." *International Peacekeeping* 16, no. 1 (2009): 115–135.

Winston, Morton. "The Humanitarian Argument for the Iraq War." *Journal of Human Rights* 4, no. 1 (2005): 45–51.

Wolf, Albert B. "After the Iran Deal: Competing Visions for Israel's Nuclear Posture." *Comparative Strategy* 35, no. 2 (2016): 124–130.

Wuthnow, Joel. "The Concept of Soft Power in China's Strategic Discourse." *Issues and Studies* 44, no. 2 (2008): 1–28.

Wynbrandt, James. *A Brief History of Saudi Arabia.* New York: Facts On File, 2010.

INDEX

Numerals

Printed in the United States
By Bookmasters